REPRINTS OF ECONOMIC CLASSICS

A COMPARATIVE VIEW
OF THE VARIOUS INSTITUTIONS FOR THE
ASSURANCE *of* LIVES

Also Published In

Reprints of Economic Classics

By CHARLES BABBAGE

ON THE ECONOMY OF MACHINERY & MANUFACTURES [1835]

A

COMPARATIVE VIEW

OF THE

VARIOUS INSTITUTIONS

FOR THE

ASSURANCE OF LIVES

BY

CHARLES BABBAGE

[1826]

REPRINTS OF ECONOMIC CLASSICS

AUGUSTUS M. KELLEY · PUBLISHERS
NEW YORK · 1967

First Edition 1826

(London: *Printed for* J. Mawman, *Ludgate-Street.*
Sold by J. Booth, *Duke-Street, Portland-Place,* 1826)

Reprinted 1967 by
AUGUSTUS M. KELLEY · PUBLISHERS

Library of Congress Catalogue Card Number
67-18568

PRINTED IN THE UNITED STATES OF AMERICA
by SENTRY PRESS, NEW YORK, N. Y. 10019

A

COMPARATIVE VIEW

OF THE VARIOUS

Institutions

FOR THE

ASSURANCE OF LIVES.

By CHARLES BABBAGE, Esq. M.A., F.R.S. L. & E.

V. P. AST. SOC. F. C. PHIL. SOC. MEMB. ACAD. DIJON, CORR. PHIL. SOC. PARIS, AND ACAD. MARSEILLES, &c. &c.

LONDON:

PRINTED FOR J. MAWMAN, LUDGATE-STREET;

AND SOLD BY

J. BOOTH, DUKE-STREET, PORTLAND-PLACE.

1826.

CONTENTS.

APPENDIX.

TO

WILLIAM WOLRYCHE WHITMORE, Esq. M.P.

&c. &c. &c.

THESE SHEETS ARE INSCRIBED,

AS

A TRIBUTE OF RESPECT

FOR

THE UNDEVIATING INDEPENDENCE OF HIS PUBLIC CONDUCT,

AND

AS A SMALL TESTIMONY OF ESTEEM

FROM

HIS FAITHFUL

AND AFFECTIONATE FRIEND,

CHARLES BABBAGE.

PREFACE.

It is a matter of very little interest to the public, to be informed of the motives which have induced me to throw together the observations contained in the following pages. I have freely canvassed the various institutions for the assurance* of

* The terms *insurance* and *assurance* have been used indiscriminately for contracts relative to life, fire, and shipping ; as custom has rather more frequently employed the latter term for those relative to life, I have in this volume entirely restricted the word *assurance* to that sense. If this distinction be admitted, *assurance* will signify a contract dependent on the duration of life, which must either happen or fail; and *insurance* will mean a contract relating to any other uncertain event which may partly happen or partly fail; thus, in adjusting the price for insurance on houses and ships, regard is always had to the chance of salvage arising from partial destruction.

life, and since I have as freely blamed those things which I thought deserving of reprobation, it is not impossible that others may assign to me motives, to which I am myself a stranger.

I think it therefore necessary merely to state that I am not in the slightest degree connected with any of them, unless an assurance of small amount with the Equitable Society may be considered as influencing my judgment with regard to that establishment. Having been induced, from several circumstances, to bestow some attention on the subject of assurances on lives, I could not help observing how very imperfectly the merits of the numerous and complicated institutions for this purpose were understood, even by persons otherwise well informed; to this circumstance may be attributed the publication of a work which has few claims either to novelty or originality. Most of its facts are already, in some shape, before the public; and having no desire to occupy my time in writing a mathematical treatise on the doctrine of annuities, I should have altogether forborne from inserting any algebraical formula, had I not been induced to believe that a few of the tables, which had been computed with some labour, might form a trifling addition to the subject.

In the "Doctrine of Life Annuities and Assurances," Mr. Baily has anticipated me in giving a sketch of the offices then existing: so many new ones have arisen since the period at which he wrote, that they require a volume rather than a chapter for their analysis. In exposing the disgraceful practices which prevail at some of them, I am merely repeating sentiments which he has more forcibly expressed: and, although his remarks have not yet had the effect of removing the evil, I feel confident that little more is requisite, than by rendering those practices generally known, to make them universally condemned.

If the reader should think that I have been too sparing of praise, too ready to criticise, let him consider that my object has been to collect and arrange information for his use, and that my criticisms may not be without value, even to the institutions which give rise to them. If, from what I have stated, he should be disinclined to become an assurer, he will have arrived at conclusions very different from my own. In my opinion, there are few situations in life in which it is not desirable, at some period or other, to enter into contracts of this kind; and on this point I quite agree with the sentiments expressed by Mr. Morgan, in the preface to his treatise on assurances.*

One conclusion, I think, naturally arises from the examination entered into of the following work, that the existing offices might be considerably improved, and that

* "I consider every assurance made for the purpose "of providing for a surviving family, in whatever office "it is effected, not only as a private but as a public "good."

notwithstanding their number, there is yet room for others: the new ones must, however, take advantage of the experience which has been accumulated; they must be perfectly explicit in all their statements; and court publicity in their accounts, as the best security for the fulfilment of their promises.

There is one mistake which I have occasionally observed, and which, as it is unjust, I should wish to remove. Persons, unable of themselves to form an estimate of the merits of an office, sometimes judge that it must be good from the known skill and ability of the actuary who conducts it; and on the other hand, if any inconsistency or impropriety in its proceedings is pointed out, the defect is almost invariably imputed to the same officer. Now, the degree of knowledge possessed by persons so situated at the different institutions, is exceedingly various, passing through all degrees, from the most superficial acquirements, derived merely from the routine of an office, up to the most profound knowledge of the subject. Unfortunately, however, for the public, the power they possess is not always equal to the weight which is due to their integrity and knowledge; and whatever may be the excellence of any regulation they propose, or the advice they offer, it is frequently neutralized by passing through the ordeal of a board of directors, far too intent upon profit, and who, in their joint capacity, esteem it no degradation to sanction measures, which they would be very sorry to be considered as acting upon in their characters as individuals.

With respect to the accuracy of the information I have collected together, I can only say that it has been the result of considerable pains and care; and that it has been my anxious desire to discuss candidly, what I have endeavoured to state correctly.

Omissions will sometimes occur, and errors occasionally mix themselves in the most carefully digested materials. The best apology I can offer for any such unintentional neglect or mistatement is, to express my readiness and desire to receive any facts or information which may come to me in an authentic form, and to correct in a subsequent edition (should such be called for) any error or omission into which I may have fallen. It is obviously necessary that all such communications should be *written;* and those who may favour me with them, are requested to leave them in the hands of my publisher.

Most of the tables were computed originally by two independent calculators, when unfortunately both copies were lost together: I have since caused them to be recalculated, some of them again twice over, and I hope they will be found correct.

Since this volume was printed, a new company, called the Ægis, has published proposals for assuring lives. It is proprietary, having a nominal capital of one million, but the public are not informed what proportion has been paid up. Its rates for the whole duration of life are nearly the same as those of the Guardian, except in a few instances, where they are one penny, and in no case more than twopence lower. No bonus is given to the assured. The minor regulations, as to the time allowed for payment of premiums, &c., are rather liberal; and the chief novelty is, that the society will at any time purchase any of its policies which have been granted for the whole duration of life, for one-third of the amount of all the premiums which may have been paid on it.

Devonshire-street, Portland-place,
26th December, 1825.

INTRODUCTION.

Nothing is more proverbially uncertain than the duration of human life, when the maxim is applied to an individual; yet there are few things less subject to fluctuation than the average duration of a multitude of individuals.

The number of deaths happening amongst persons of our own acquaintance, is frequently very different in different years; and it is not an uncommon event that this number shall be double, treble, or even many times larger in one year than in the next succeeding. If we consider larger societies ot individuals as the inhabitants of a village or small town, the number of deaths is more uniform; and in still larger bodies, as among the inhabitants of a kingdom, the uniformity is such, that the excess of deaths in any year above the average number seldom exceeds a small fractional part of the whole.*

This fluctuation may be confined within still smaller limits if we exclude from the enumeration those portions of the population which are most exposed to the casual effects of disease or want, during seasons when the supply of food is scanty; and if there existed any data by which we might separate the effects arising from deaths amongst the young and the poor, there are good grounds for presuming that the variations from the mean would be yet very considerably reduced.

It may be a curious matter of inquiry, to

* In the two periods, each of fifteen years, beginning at 1780, the number of deaths occurring in England and Wales in any year did not fall short of, or exceed the average number, one-thirteenth part of the whole: nor did the number dying in any one year differ from the number of those dying in the next by a tenth part.

persons who have not considered the subject, to compare the deviations from the average of mortality with the deviations from the average price of commodities, and of no little surprise to find the result in favour of the equality of the average of mortality.

In order to show more clearly this fact, I have subjoined the following tables :—

	Deaths.	Price of Wheat.				Deaths.	Price of Wheat.		
		£	s.	d.			£	s.	d.
1780	198,348	1	15	8	1795	210,339	3	14	2
1	195,902	2	4	8	6	190,897	3	17	1
2	187,152	2	7	10	7	191,306	2	13	1
3	188,264	2	12	8	8	187,531	2	10	3
4	194,401	2	8	10	9	189,586	3	7	6
5	191,866	2	11	10	1800	208,063	5	13	7
6	185,232	1	18	10	1	204,434	5	18	3
7	184,881	2	1	2	2	199,889	3	7	5
8	187,598	2	5	0	3	203,728	2	16	6
9	185,570	2	11	2	4	181,177	3	0	1
1790	184,894	2	13	2	5	181,240	4	7	0
1	186,674	2	7	0	6	183,452	3	19	0
2	188,906	2	2	11	7	195,851	3	13	3
3	203,653	2	8	11	8	200,763	3	19	0
4	197,740	2	11	8	9	191,471	4	15	7

Average annual price during 15 years, ending 1797, of		Highest Average of same during any one Year.	Greatest variations per cent. above Average.
Wheat, qr.	s. 41.7	75	82.2
Tallow, cwt.	s. 45	66	46.7
W.I. Sugar, cwt.	s. 38.7	63	62.8
Irish Beef, tierce	s. 84	102.5 £	22 0
English Pig Iron, ton . .	s. 90	126	40.0
Hops, cwt.	s. 96	176	83.3
English Linseed, tun, oil .	35£	48.5 £	38.6
Coffee W.I., cwt.	s. 87.8	115	31.0
Copper, cwt.	s. 91	114.5	25.8
Mortality during 15 years ending 1797			10·0
Mortality during 15 years ending 1810			7·0

The average annual price of three per cents. during fifteen years, ending 1797, was £70; the highest average of same during any one year £84; the greatest variation above average price, 20.0 per cent.

The average number of persons dying annually in England during fifteen years, ending in 1797, was 191,481; the greatest variation above the average was ten per cent.

The annual average of fifteen years, ending in 1810, was 194,505; the greatest variation above the average was seven per cent.

The first of these tables* contains the number of burials in England and Wales

* The first table was extracted from the work of Mr. Milne on annuities, and the second was abstracted from the valuable collection of tables at the end of Mr. Tooke's work on high and low prices.

during thirty years, and also the average price of wheat per quarter for each year. Dividing it into two periods of fifteen years each, we find in the first the average number of deaths annually to be 190,725, differing from the largest annual number, 203,653, by 12,928, or nearly one-fifteenth. In the second period the average annual number of deaths is 194,648, which differs from the greatest, 210,339, by 15,691, or about one-twelfth. Whilst in the first fifteen years the average price of corn was 2*l.* 6*s.* 9*d.*, which differs from the greatest by 6*s.* 5*d.*, or almost one-seventh: and in the second period the mean annual price was 3*l.* 16*s.* 9*d.*, which differs from the greatest by 2*l.* 1*s.* 6*d.*, or more than one-half.

The second table contains the average annual price for fifteen years of many articles of very general consumption, (both of domestic and of foreign produce;) the second column contains the average price during the whole period; the third the highest annual average price; and the fourth expresses the rate per cent. of the greatest variation above the average price. The difference which exists in the magnitude of these deviations from the mean price of these commodities, sufficiently proves that it cannot be caused by any variations in the currency in which they are expressed. It can therefore only arise from the difference of the supply or production of them.

The number of annual deaths amongst the population of this country seldom exceeds the average above ten per cent.,* whilst the excess above the average price

* This statement is not intended to apply to other countries, where small-pox and epidemics, added, perhaps, to habits unfavourable to health and want of sufficient medical skill, concur in rendering the average far more uncertain. Thus, in Sweden, a country which has been subject to frequent seasons of scarcity, as well as to ravages from small-pox, the three periods of fifteen years each, succeeding 1750, give for the deviations from the mean 29, 64, and 24 per cent. Yet even here, where the influence of the same circumstances are extended over a larger space of time, the regularity of nature is

of the least fluctuating of the commodities just mentioned, amounts to twenty-five per cent.; and in most of the other instances it reaches a much greater extent.

Another important consequence may be deduced from the comparison which has been instituted: since the fluctuation in the price of life, arising from the natural uncertainty of its duration, is considerably less than that which occurs in the price of most commodities, a person who deals in securities dependent on lives, requires less capital to carry on his business than one who trades to an equal extent in any other species of merchandise to which we have referred.

It will, perhaps, be urged that the value of contingencies depending on lives, varies with the rate of interest which money will produce: this is undoubtedly correct; but, since it is usual in all such transactions to

very remarkable. The number of births during the same three periods differed from the average 4.1, 14.1, and 12.6 per cent.

assume as the basis of the calculation that money will only produce three per cent., which is nearly, if not quite, the lowest rate that has occurred for any considerable interval, the argument which is maintained, that *the variations in the rate of mortality require but little capital to meet them*, remains unimpaired.

The system of a mutual assurance society, in one of its simplest forms, may be illustrated by supposing it to consist of one thousand persons, each aged twenty and in good health, and with such certificates of a good constitution as the Equitable Society would admit. Each individual should pay 1*l*. 9*s*. 6*d*., to receive 100*l*. on his death. The premiums at the end of the first year, increased by the interest on them, would amount to 1468*l*.; and the payments to be made on account of six deaths, being deducted, would leave 868*l*. At the commencement of the second year the 994 payments of 1*l*. 9*s*. 6*d*. each, added to the 868*l*., would produce 2334*l*., which at the end of the year would amount to 2404*l.*; from this the claims due from the average number of deaths being subtracted would leave 1804*l.* The 988 payments of the next year added to this sum would, at the end of the third year, after deducting six claims, produce 2759*l.* The capital of the society at the end of the first, second, and third years would be as follows :—

At the end of the 1st year	868*l.*	after paying	600*l.*	claims.
2d year	1804*l.*	do.	600*l.*	do.
3d year	2759*l.*	do.	600*l.*	do.
&c.	&c.			

For many years this capital would continue to increase, until the sum arising from the diminished number of contributors would exactly pay the number of the annual claimants. After this, the annual income arising from the premiums being insufficient to pay the annual claims, a portion of the accumulated capital must each year be taken to make up the sum required for that purpose, until after about eighty years; when the remains of this fund, together with the premium paid at the beginning of the last year, will be just sufficient to pay the last claim.

In this outline it is taken for granted, that the deaths will occur precisely as the experience of the Equitable Society has indicated: the larger the number of the assurers the greater is the probability that this will happen, and the extent of the deviations would perhaps be but small.

There is one mistake which ought to be guarded against, and which is not unfrequent; it arises from considering the capital accumulated, and in the possession of the society at any period, as so much profit: thus, at the end of the third year it possesses 2759*l.*; but no part of this is profit, for if the value of the policies of each of the 988 persons remaining were computed by the same table as that from which the premium was determined, their total amount would be precisely equal to this sum, added to the value of the annuities owed to the society by those persons.

The very general prevalence of this mistake, even amongst well-informed persons, must be my apology for dwelling on it longer than it might otherwise seem to require. It is an error at once injurious to the societies, and dangerous to the public. The following is one of those arguments proposed as favourable to the formation of a University Life Assurance Society :—

" On these data,* if each of the members (of the University Club) had assured his life for 1000*l.*, on the formation of that establishment, at the rates usually demanded by assurance offices, the amount of premiums for three years would have been about 90,000*l.*, and the amount of losses only 38,000*l.*"

Was it intended by this paragraph that the reader should infer that in such circumstances the society would make a

* The data will become the subject of inquiry in a future page.

profit of 52,000*l.* in the three years? This was, I understand, the sense in which some of its members apprehended it. Yet it is difficult to conceive that such a confusion between capital accumulated to meet future demands, and a realized profit, could exist in the minds of those whose names are connected with that institution; some of whom are well known to possess a far more profound and extensive acquaintance with mathematical science, than the limited nature of these subjects would demand. Yet, if such were not the interpretation, it is equally difficult to conjecture the reason of their submitting to the members of the Universities a piece of information almost as instructive as half the enunciation of some geometrical theorem, or the first term of some unfinished syllogism.

In the original constitution of the Equitable Society it was provided, that the total value of all the outstanding policies should be ascertained annually, and that whenever it exceeded the capital accumulated, such a call should be made on each of the assurers, as would, when their sum was added to the capital, make it equal to all the engagements to which it was pledged; and, on the other hand, whenever the demands were less in value than this capital, the surplus was to be immediately divided amongst the assurers. This plan of immediately dividing the profits was abandoned at an early period after the establishment of that institution.

If we now suppose that the sum annually paid by each of the thousand assurers had been one-third larger, or 1*l.* 19*s.* 4*d.* each, which is less than many assurance companies at present charge, then, besides the sums already mentioned, the society would possess

At the end of the 1st year	- - -	489*l.*
2d year	- - -	1007*l.*
3d year	- - -	1538*l.*
&c. &c.		

The annual payments, before the additional third was taken, were sufficient to form a fund which would exactly pay all the policies as they became claims, and itself be exhausted on the payment of the last. If, therefore, the deaths took place in the manner supposed, no further sum of money would be required to meet all the demands, and these additional sums would be really profit; and, unlike the former, they will continue to increase until the last claim is paid.

At the termination of this society of mutual assurers there will, therefore, remain a large unappropriated capital.

On comparing these sums with the probable amount of claims in the three first years, it will be seen that if their real had been double their probable amount, the society could have paid them, and yet have remained in a state equal to meet all its demands.

The extreme improbability of such an occurrence may be estimated from what has been previously stated relative to the fluctuations in the rate of mortality.

A society taking such premiums would, therefore, in a very few years, have a large excess of capital more than sufficient to protect its members against any irregularity in the rate of their mortality; and part of which might, at periodical intervals, be distributed amongst them in the form of a bonus.

In the above illustration, for the sake of greater simplicity, we have considered a society constituted, at the beginning, of a number of persons all of the same age; this can rarely or never happen, if the numbers of such a society are at all considerable. The results will however be the same, if any member, who is above the standard age, pay to the general fund such an increased premium as will exactly compensate the chance of his dying sooner, in consequence of his increased age; and, if this is true for one person, it will be so for any number. It is therefore immaterial what the different ages of the subscribers may be, provided they *each pay a premium exactly proportioned to their chance of dying*. The difficulty which now arises is, therefore, to calculate a table of rates which shall give this fair proportion of payments for different ages.

All reasoning and all calculation, which is to be employed in the practical purposes of life, must ultimately rest on facts. In the infancy of those transactions, of which the present volume treats, when the facts were in some measure doubtful, and the data insufficient, and when it was not known how little or how much the rate of mortality deviated from itself, it was prudent to take a much larger sum in the shape of premium, to cover such risks, than it is now necessary to require, when an extensive collection of facts has given rise to a more enlarged knowledge.

Five pounds were at first demanded as the price of assuring a hundred pounds for one year, on a life of any age; and at one establishment, middle-aged or old lives were not taken even on these terms. This sum was probably fixed upon from its appearing that the annual number of deaths in London was nearly one in twenty of the population. It must soon have occurred to those who wished to have recourse to such transactions, that the chance of a person aged twenty dying within any given period, could not be so great as that of a person of forty dying within the same limit; and, consequently, that it was not equitable to demand the same rate of premium in both cases. And it must also have appeared, that if a table of the number of persons, amongst a considerable population, dying annually at the different ages of life, could be procured, by its means the relative chances of life of persons of different ages might be assigned. This introduced the reference to bills of mortality—a great step; even when the imperfect nature of the materials on which they depended is taken into the account.

A COMPARATIVE VIEW, *&c.*

CHAPTER I.

Of the Tables of Mortality employed for calculating the Premiums of Assurances.

In order to determine the proper annual sum which should be paid by a person of a given age assuring 100*l.* payable at his death, it is requisite that we should know, out of a given number of persons similarly circumstanced, (suppose ten thousand,) the number of those who would die in the first year, the number dying in the second and third years, until they all became extinct. In the absence of such tables, the Equitable Society, which was established in 1762, determined the payments they required for different ages from a table constructed by Simpson and Dodson, I believe, from the number dying at each age in London. After the experience of fourteen years it was found that these premiums were too high, and they were therefore reduced. During the five following years, the number of deaths amongst the members of the society was so much fewer than the tables of observations supposed them to be, that it was thought expedient to have recourse to a table of observations which gave more correct values of the duration of human life. The observations at Northampton were accordingly employed, and fifteen per cent. was added to the premiums computed from them. During the course of the next five years it was observed, that the number of deaths amongst the members of the Equitable Society, was much less than that amongst an equal number of persons in the metropolis, or even in the small town of Northampton; and the fifteen per cent., which had hitherto been added to the premium deduced from the Northampton observations, was no longer taken.

Each reduction was preceded by a minute inquiry into the affairs of the Society; and the prudent caution with which these successive amendments were adopted is much to be admired. The last change in their premiums took place in the year 1786. Nearly forty years have since elapsed, and it is sincerely to be hoped that science which, by pointing out the legitimate use of experience, guided them in their earliest progress and secured their prosperity, may continue to direct the course of an institution now approaching its maturity without a rival, and which has contributed so largely to the good of the community. I should be sorry that it should be inferred from these remarks, that each addition of experience and each new inquiry should produce a diminution of the premiums; a limit must necessarily be found, beyond which it would be imprudent to proceed; how nearly that limit is yet approached, we shall be better able to judge when I have placed more information before my readers; and to whatever conclusions the same evidence may lead different minds, I think all will agree that the *premiums paid for the assurance of the same sum, on an old and on a young life, should be as nearly proportioned to the real risks as the state of our knowledge will admit.*

The table formed from observations on the duration of human life amongst the inhabitants of Northampton, has for several years been the basis of the premiums taken by many of the assurance offices. More lately, the observations on the mortality which occurs amongst the inhabitants of Carlisle have, with certain modifications, been employed by a few; and I am not aware that any other tables, of known reputation, have ever been distinctly stated to be employed for the same purpose.

The fair sum to be paid annually for an assurance on a given life, must depend on two circumstances: the rate of mortality amongst the class to which the person assured belongs; and the interest which will probably be made of money during the continuance of those annual payments. As the latter of these circumstances is subject to continual fluctuation, it has been usual to make the calculation at three per cent.; a rate highly favourable to the offices, since it is nearly the lowest which has ever occurred for any considerable time. It has been the practice of the Equitable Society, which has been followed by nearly all the other offices, to employ a table in which the rate of mortality is greater than that amongst its members, and calculating the premiums from it, supposing the interest of money to be always three per cent., to add nothing to them in the shape of profit. Yet the profits which result from these transactions are immense; and they arise from the average rate of interest being greater than that which was assumed, and from the number of deaths amongst the assured being less than those occurring amongst an equal number of persons of all classes, indiscriminately taken in a large town.

This method of determining the premiums to be taken is, in the present state of our knowledge, both inexpedient and unscientific, although when first employed it deserved a very different character. I imagine it will not require much argument to show, that the more proper course would be, to determine, as nearly as we can, the real value of the risk, and consequently the amount of premium just sufficient to meet it, and to add to this such a per centage as will defray the expenses of management, and allow of a sufficient dividend to the proprietors, whose capital is a guarantee to the assured.

This plan might be adopted even by those who think the present premiums sufficiently low, and the only result would be to render more equitable the relative premiums paid on lives of different ages, and to give a clearer insight into the affairs of the society.

Reserving the question relative to the interest of money for a future page, I shall at present assume, that it increases at the rate of three per cent., and now inquire into the best method of determining the risk of life. If we were to take indiscriminately from all classes of a large population, ten thousand infants just born, and were to note how many of these die in the first, second, third, &c., and in each succeeding year, until they are all extinct, a table so formed, would enable us to ascertain the true value of a life of any age, taken without selection from the same population. It must, however, be remembered that at any period, suppose when only six thousand of these remain alive, perhaps at the age of twenty, the value of a life given by this table, is not the value of a healthy life of twenty, but of a person having the average state of health of those at that time in existence. Some few of these may be at the point of death, and several will be in such a state as to die in the next and succeeding years. But at all the insurance offices the nominee is warranted to be in good health at the time of the contract being made; and, on this ground alone, we ought to expect a much smaller mortality amongst that class of persons, than amongst the general population of a country. Another circumstance, which contributes much to diminish the rate of mortality amongst the assured, is, that they are all selected from the middle and higher ranks of society, and are consequently exempt from many sources of unhealthiness to which the poor are liable.

The effect of several trades and species of labour is very prejudicial to the health of those immediately employed in them; and each of these will exert an influence on the results of the general tables, proportional to the degree of injury it produces in the constitution, and to the number of those engaged in it.

Seasons of scarcity affect materially the health of the poor; but the class who make assurances are generally placed beyond their influence.

As the offices seldom assure lives under fifteen, they are not liable to the irregularities which affect the earliest years of life; nor are such lives exposed to those disorders which usually occur in childhood.

Another reason for the diminished rate of mortality amongst assurers is, that those who have not had the small-pox, or who have had certain disorders which are likely to produce danger by their recurrence, are excluded. I am not acquainted with any data to which we can recur, in order to appreciate the risks arising from each of these sources separately. With regard to the small-pox, however, it has been shown by M. Duvillard, that the introduction of vaccination has increased the mean duration of human life about three years and a half: and he has computed tables, from which the risk, arising from the chance, that a person who has not been inoculated or vaccinated shall die of the small-pox, may be known for any age.

Persons who have had the gout are not usually assured on the same terms as others; to what degree it has a tendency to shorten life, is not perhaps well determined; the additional premium which is demanded by the offices, of about 10*l*.* per cent., computed on the premiums, most probably is found sufficient for the risk. Insanity forms another ground of exclusion; nor are persons subject to fits of any kind accepted. Rupture is, with most of the offices, a ground of rejection; probably it has not much influence on the class of assurers, who, from their situation in life, are not exposed to the constant efforts of bodily exertion, on which the existence of the lower classes almost solely depends.

* At the Equitable Society, the premiums of those who have not had the small-pox, nor been vaccinated, or who *have had* the gout, are increased by eleven per cent. Persons who have been vaccinated are admitted on the usual terms; but if they die of the small-pox, their policy becomes void. See Regulation of Dec. 1802.

Every office requires a declaration that the person assured is not subject to any disease tending to shorten life; and they are further protected, by a similar assurance from two persons (one generally medical) well acquainted with the assured, who also certify their belief that the party is not addicted to any habits tending to shorten life. There occurs to me but one circumstance which is likely to counterbalance these various sources of security, that the lives assured shall possess the average degree of health. It is true, indeed, that self-interest is a powerful motive; and it is stated, that many persons, believing or knowing themselves to be likely not to live long, go to the offices and effect policies on their lives, with the view of benefiting their families. That such cases sometimes occur, I am ready to admit, and that those which come to the knowledge of the public, by being contested, can only be the most flagrant; yet, I believe their occurrence to be, on the whole, comparatively rare. The great mass of assurers are those who can devote a part of the surplus of their incomes to the purpose of rendering, in some measure, permanent, an income dependent on their lives. It should also be observed, that those who are least sanguine in their expectations of a lengthened existence, are not always amongst the most short-lived; and that if such a belief is occasionally the inducement to a few to assure their lives, many of them will, in all probability, live to perceive the fallacy of their opinions, and to pay an ample price for the benefits they had prematurely anticipated for their families. The fortunate exposure of one or two such cases, has done much to prove, even to the most selfish, that such conduct is not quite safe, and that whilst the moral guilt must be incurred at the commencement, the distant profit is not altogether so certain. The better lives generally go to the more respectable offices; and many which are rejected by these are accepted at other offices, where, from the disadvantageous nature of the terms to the assured, they are glad to accept lives of a less select description.

It appears that many and powerful circumstances combine to render the rate of mortality, among a select class of assurers, much less than that which occurs amongst the inhabitants of large towns; and admitting to the counteracting cause more weight than, in my own opinion, it deserves, still I think the reasons already stated, namely, the healthy state of the life at the time of making the contract; the class of society in which assurers are found exempting them from sources of unhealthiness occurring among the poor; the rejection of those who have not had the small-pox; of those who have had the gout or fits, and several other complaints; and, finally, the declaration of the party, corroborated by that of two friends, that he is not subject to any disease tending to shorten life, and that he is not in the practice of habits calculated to produce the same effect; strongly preponderate, and from their joint action we ought to expect, that the law of mortality, amongst a body of persons so selected, should differ considerably from that which takes place in a large country.

It is therefore to be expected, that the law of mortality which exists amongst assurers, should approach more nearly to that which takes place amongst select classes of mankind, such as amongst annuitants, (where it is the interest of each proprietor to select a good life,) than to more indiscriminate bodies of people. Although there exist good observations of this kind, I am not aware of their having been employed as the basis of any table of premiums for assurances.

Having now pointed out the defects of the tables in general use, it will naturally be inquired what others it is proposed to substitute. To this it may be answered, that the best substitution would be a table actually constructed from the deaths occurring amongst a large body of persons of this very class, whose law of mortality we wish to ascertain. Materials for such a table exist, and probably in the best and most authentic form. The Equitable Society has been established sixty years, and it must possess records of the death, and cause of death, of all those who have had claims on its funds. Another society of considerable extent, the Amicable, has existed above a century. A vast quantity of valuable materials is, without doubt, contained in the records of these two societies; and if they were each to communicate to the public the facts of which they are in possession, it would form a most important addition to our knowledge, and supply the most accurate materials for tables of this class which have yet been produced. It is a fortunate circumstance that the two institutions, in which are deposited this great accumulation of facts, are unfettered by the partial and contending interest of any proprietary. Founded alike for the mutual benefit of all who choose to become members, they have each pursued their separate course, diffusing comfort and security over a multitude of families: they form, as it were, a portion of the public; and there are no private interests to oppose their publishing, for the advancement of science, the results of that experience, which it alone, by securing their stability, has enabled them to acquire; thus supplying the solid materials of further reasonings, and further improvements, which must inevitably reflect back the greatest advantages on those most largely engaged in such transactions. In the absence of that which would, undoubtedly, be the best data for the construction of such tables, I have had recourse to a very valuable substitute, for which the public are indebted to Mr. Morgan; it consists of the comparative decrements of life, between the experience of the Equitable Society and the Northampton tables. The comparison is instituted for every ten years; and although it would have been more valuable had it referred to shorter periods, yet, I believe, when they are published, it will not be found to differ widely from the more numerous and detailed results; and, I have no doubt, that it will more nearly represent the actual state of mortality amongst such a body of persons, than any other table. By the aid of this table I have computed the value of an annuity on lives of different ages, and also the annual premium for the assurance of 100*l.*, supposing nothing to be added for the expenses of management, or profits of any kind. This latter table will be found highly useful for comparing the rate of profit charged on all such contracts by the different societies.

The experience of the Equitable Society, during the thirty years which terminated in 1800, has furnished the data; and the confidence which I repose in their accuracy is confirmed by the statement of Mr. Morgan,* that "the probabilities of life appear to have been equally favourable in every period."

* Address of Mr. Morgan to the Equitable Society, 1801.

CHAP. II.

Of the average Rate of the Interest of Money.

After a correct table of the decrements of human life has been formed, it is necessary, before it can be employed as the basis of the calculations for assurance companies, to compute from it tables at such a rate of interest as that at which the society is likely to increase its funds.

In order to give an advantage to the offices, it has usually been assumed, that the rate of interest which can be procured for money is three per cent. This rate it was prudent to adopt when such kinds of contracts were first introduced: but it well deserves consideration, whether it is not at the present time more prudent to adopt another rate better adapted to the real average. If a rate of assurance at all ages is calculated at three per cent., and money is improved by the office at five per cent., the effect is not merely to increase the profits of the office equally on all lives; but it will be found that, in such circumstances, the profits derived from the premiums on the younger lives will have increased much faster than those on the older. Thus, by the Northampton table used at the Equitable, the profit made on a life aged fifty, is to that as one aged twenty, by their own experience.

In the ratio of	100 : 164	of money produces	$2\frac{1}{2}$ per cent.
	100 : 172		3 per cent.
	100 : 183		4 per cent.
	100 : 233		5 per cent.

From this circumstance it may happen that a set of tables, in which the probability of life for the younger ages is underrated, may be made to agree nearly with a more correct table, if the values of assurances deduced from the latter are calculated at a lower rate of interest. Thus the price given by the Equitable for additions to its policies, is calculated from the Northampton tables at four per cent.; and it does not much differ from the value computed from its own experience at three per cent.

When it is considered that the average age of persons who assure is about forty-seven, as will be hereafter shown, one of the inducements for using a low rate of interest becomes manifest.

There is, however, an inconvenience which is likely to arise from employing a rate much below the average, which is, that it renders any prospective consideration of the concerns of a society liable to great deviations from the truth. These will, it is true, be on the safe side; but it is much better to calculate what is likely to be a near approximation, and then make a sufficient allowance, than to make use of a rule which gives an allowance, with whose magnitude we are unacquainted.

With the view of getting some approximation to the average rate of interest in this country, I have examined a period of ninety-two years of peace and war, commencing at 1731, and terminating in 1822. By extracting from the tables collected and published by M. Cæsar Moreau,* the highest and lowest price of the three per

* The data were extracted from the valuable "Chart of British Trade," by Cæsar Moreau, Esq.

cents. during each year, it appears that the average annual price was

73·1 during 48 years of war.
86·14 during 44 years of peace.
79·33 during 92 years of war and peace.

These averages are deduced from the mean of the highest and lowest prices during each year; more numerous observations might alter them a little, but they are sufficiently accurate for the present purpose. The rates of interest that these averages would indicate are

4·1 per cent. during war.
3·48 per cent. during peace.
3·78 per cent. during war and peace.

If it be considered that it is generally possible, without additional risk, to make rather a higher rate of interest than that which is yielded by the three per cents., it seems reasonable to conclude, that four per cent. annually is about the rate of interest which an establishment, calculated for any considerable duration, may expect to make.

CHAP. III.

Of the different Kinds of Societies for the Assurance of Lives.

The various institutions for the assurance of lives, are constituted on three different plans. In some of these all the assurers for the whole term of life are mutually responsible; they participate in the profits, and are subject to calls to replace any loss or deficiency in their funds. In some of those now existing, in which this system has been adopted, a large surplus fund has been accumulated and reserved out of the profits, which renders this responsibility merely nominal, since the chances against its being necessary to enforce it are remote in the highest degree. I hope, however, that it has been clearly established in the preceding pages, that a large capital at the commencement is quite unnecessary; and that it will be conceded that, in a business in which the receipts are paid long before any demands take place, and where, consequently, there can occur no losses from bad debts, a failure can only arise by an improvident consumption of the funds, or by employing a table of premiums inadequate to the risks undertaken. Considerable uncertainty has lately prevailed relative to the extent of the responsibility incurred by the proprietors in joint-stock companies ; and associations for the mutual assurances of life, although differing in several essential respects, have fallen under the same doubts. To such an extent have these been carried, urged partly by opinions of high authority, and partly perhaps by the assertions of rival offices, that the validity of the commonest transactions has been doubted. It will scarcely be credited some few years hence, should these pages survive, that, in the year in which I write,* such was the uncertainty of the law, or such the state of public opinion, that well-informed and sensible persons seriously questioned whether,

* This was written in the year 1824.

if two parties entered into a written agreement on a subject not forbidden by any law, the one to purchase, the other to contract a certain limited responsibility precisely specified in the document, the law might not interfere, and compel the one to incur a greater responsibility than the other had paid for. Such was the case, not in one, nor in two, but in numerous instances, and I have even heard the policy of such an interference defended. On this latter question, connected as it is with other and widely different institutions, I shall not enter.

The mischief which arises from uncertainty I have myself witnessed; and should more general views justify the adoption of any principle, forbidding a responsibility to a limited extent, there will be no injustice, provided it be known, and do not act retrospectively. One of its consequences will be, that the assured, being compelled to accept from the companies a larger share of responsibility than he himself thinks necessary for his security, will be obliged to pay for it an additional price; and thus the general rate on which policies on lives can be effected will, as far as this cause operates, be raised.

Considering the great extent of property dependent on assurances on lives, and the good policy of fostering such a disposition to prudence and foresight in the people, it seems desirable that questions of this nature should be set at rest. And that the important benefit of this branch of domestic expenditure is well understood by the government, appears sufficiently attested by the circumstance, that, during the greatest pressure of our financial difficulties, no attempt was made to raise a tax on the large amount of premiums annually paid; an event which, had it taken place, would have effectually retarded their increase.

The importance of the subject will, I hope, be admitted as an excuse for this digression from the more immediate object of this section. Of societies founded on the principle of mutual assurance, there are established in London the four following:—

The Amicable,	London Life Assurance,
Equitable,	Norwich Life.

The second principle on which institutions of this kind are founded, is that of a number of persons forming a company, and raising a capital, usually in transferable shares, to guarantee the payment of all policies they effect: the advantages of such institutions are supposed to consist in the superior security to the assured, and in the absence of all responsibility, which it is admitted in this case cannot attach to them. The exact sums agreed upon are paid on the deaths of the assured, without any deductions or additions. The rates of those offices which adopt this plan are generally high; and it may deserve consideration whether the additional security is not dearly purchased at such a price as is usually required by these companies. The following are the names of those which have adopted this plan:—

Albion,	Pelican,
British Commercial,	Royal Exchange,
Eagle,	Sun,
Globe,	West of England,
London Assurance,	Westminster.

The third principle on which assurance companies are conducted, results from a combination of the two former. A number of proprietors subscribe together a large capital, and agree to relieve the assured from all loss and responsibility, and at stated intervals they give to the assured a certain portion of the profits which the business has produced in the interval. Whether it is legally possible to exempt those, who share in any proportion the profits of a trade, from all responsibility in case losses occur, is still viewed as a doubtful point by many of the best informed persons. Some, however, of the offices which do not make any return of profits, have boldly undertaken to decide this point, and their dictum is,—that it is impossible.

I shall now endeavour to point out the principal reasons which induce persons to assure their own lives or the lives of others, and shall suggest a few modifications of some of the methods of assuring, which might with advantage be introduced.

Assurances for short periods are usually had recourse to by those who expect to receive sums of money, provided the party on whom its receipt depends shall live one, two, or a given number of years. A sum of money is frequently given by will to a particular individual on his attaining a certain age: marriage, the birth of children, or a variety of circumstances, may render it highly desirable for that individual to have the power of disposing of that money, even though he should die before it becomes his. By assuring his life for the intervening period, this may be accomplished; for should he live to receive it, he will only have paid a moderate premium for his security; and should he die, although the original sum will take another destination from that which he intended, yet the office at which he was assured will pay to his executors an equal sum.

The same method will also facilitate his raising money on the expected payment of the legacy, should it be required for any advantageous purpose. A creditor who is secure of receiving his money, provided his debtor lives a few years, may, by assuring his life for that term, prevent the possibility of losing it. A case which frequently occurs is, that of a person just entering into possession of an entailed estate, who wishes to raise a sum of money which he can gradually repay in the next five or seven years; by assuring his life at an expense, probably, of one or two per cent., he is enabled to secure the repayment, even though he should die in the interval.

Persons engaged in any undertaking, the success of which depends on their own personal exertions, and the profit from which will necessarily be delayed for a year or two, will be well repayed the trifling expense of assuring their own lives for that term, by the relief which it will afford them from much mental anxiety; a circumstance which cannot fail to have a beneficial effect on the progress of their undertaking.

In cases where the possession of property depends on the circumstance of one person dying before or after another, it is frequently of great importance to make a provision against the occurrence of the unfortunate event. This is a contingency to which landed property is frequently subject. The heir to an estate which depends on his surviving an aged relative, wishes to make a provision for some of his family or friends : this can be best accomplished by having recourse to an assurance office. The difference in price (when there is a great disparity of years between the parties) from that of an absolute assurance is sometimes very considerable.

The great mass of the business, however, which is carried on by the numerous assurance companies, consists in assuring sums of money to be paid absolutely on the death of the respective nominees : the annual amount of money received on this account is many times larger than that which arises from all the other transactions united.

This mode of providing against those losses which arise from the uncertain tenure of human existence, is adapted to almost every class of society. All those who have any portion of their income dependent on their own exertions, or who are tenants for life of property of which they cannot dispose after their death, have recourse to this as the most ready mode of securing to their relatives, at their decease, sums of money proportionate to their means.

Thus all those, either in private or public offices, who receive an annual income for their services, may, by reserving out of their expenditure a small portion for an assurance on their life, be able at their death to dispose of a sum, which it would have required very many years to accumulate from the same annual saving.

It constantly happens that persons are disinclined from laying aside annually a small sum, from the consideration of the length of time which must elapse before it can arrive at any considerable amount. Thus a person aged twenty-five, possessing an income of 400*l.* a year, would, if he were to lay aside annually 24*l.*, and improve it at five per cent. compound interest, at the end of ten years find himself possessed of little more than 300*l.*: the same sum of 24*l.* employed in assuring his life, would enable him to dispose by will of 1000*l.*, and he would enjoy that power from the payment of the first premium.

Another case which constantly gives rise

to assurances is, that of the possessor of a lifehold estate wishing to change it into a perpetuity of smaller annual value.—Suppose a person aged twenty-seven, having an income of 400*l.* a-year, and the interest of money to be four per cent.; then, if he divide his income into two portions of 246*l.* and 154*l.*, and if with this latter he assures his life, his income will be 246*l.* a-year, and on his death the offices will pay 6150*l.*, which, at four per cent., will produce to his executors rather more than 246*l.* a-year.*

Assurance on life is frequently had recourse to as a method of saving money;

* If i = a person's annual income which will terminate with his life, and if a = the price of assuring 100*l.* on that life at any office, and r = the rate of interest which money will produce; then if he wish to reduce his income, so that at his death his executors may receive a sum whose annual interest is equal to that reduced income, he must expend in assurance annually

$$\frac{a\,i}{100\,r + a},$$

and his reduced income will be

$$i - \frac{a\,i}{100\,r + a} = \frac{100\,r\,i}{100\,r + a}.$$

This supposes the assurance to be made at an office which gives no returns of profit, a choice which few will be so improvident as to make.

and in this point of view it has its advantages, although they do not seem to be very clearly understood. Supposing the uncertainty of life to be altogether put out of the question, that is to say, admitting that a given individual will attain the average number of years which his age, at the time of forming such arrangements, entitles him to expect to reach; then it will in general be more advantageous for him to accumulate his annual savings, than to assure even at the best offices. If at the Equitable, for example, he pays more than the risk requires, all his copartners do the same, and, as they share the profits amongst them, he is not a gainer on this point. If the interest of money should be greater than three per cent., the society will make a larger profit than they calculated; but so also will the individual accumulate his own annual savings at a greater rate; consequently, on this ground, there is no advantage in assuring.

The reasons which are favourable to the plan of employing the annual surplus in an assurance are, that the office, besides transacting the business of the copartnership, acts as a trading company, and makes temporary assurances on the lives of those who do not participate in the profits; the gain which arises from this species of trade is shared among the partners or assurers for the whole term of life. To what sum this annually amounts at the Equitable, I am unable to say; but it would, I think, contribute to the credit of that establishment, already so high, if this, as well as every other particular relating to its transactions, were annually laid before the public, or at least circulated amongst ALL its members. To whatever sum this may have amounted, it can hardly be supposed it can in future be very large, since the Economic and some other offices have offered to the public so much lower terms.

Another source of profit to societies arises from assurances neglected to be continued, and the policies thus becoming forfeited; this also is much on the decline. As in a commercial country the value of such things soon becomes known, when the owner finds it inconvenient to continue his payments, he will sell at any price rather than forfeit his policy altogether. In opposition to these sources of profit, we must place the expense of the management of the institutions, which, although small at the Equitable, is considerable at many other offices. This source of expense is altogether avoided in the case of a person directing the application of his own annual savings.

There is however another advantage in making an assurance as a mode of saving, which may, in some instances, be of considerable importance, although its precise weight must depend on the character of the individual having recourse to it. When a person resolves, annually, to lay aside a certain portion of his income to accumulate at compound interest, he has, after a few years, always a fund to which, on extraordinary occasions, he can apply; and if any temptation of luxury, or any unexpected expense, should present itself, it is much more probable that he will encroach on this fund, than resist the one or supply the other by a diminution in a different branch of his expenditure. If, on the contrary, he had employed the same sum in an annual premium for an assurance, it would require some time to elapse before he could dispose of his policy to advantage, and to whatever inconvenience he might be put, his premiums would, probably, be the last disbursement that he would allow to remain unpaid.

This argument rests partly on the difficulty of getting, at a short notice, a fair price for a policy of some years' standing; a difficulty which I shall propose afterwards to remove. The inconsistency is, however, only an apparent one: on the whole, I believe it to be more advantageous to make the value of a policy known, and its property transferable to the greatest extent; and it will be easy for those, who, feeling conscious of their inability to withstand temptation, wish not to possess so ready and immediate a mode of parting with their policy, to have that clause in it omitted, which is, to bind the office to purchase it at a certain price, or else to allow some friend to hold it in trust for their use.

It is manifest that one portion of those who assure, dying sooner than they were entitled to expect, must receive from the society more money than they have contributed; and, consequently, that another portion, living longer than they could have anticipated from their age at entering, must, at their decease, receive less than they have contributed : it is on the balance of these two circumstances that these institutions are founded. Having stated the various reasons which may be urged for or against assuring, when viewed as a method of saving money, I shall now give a table for the age of twenty-five, showing the sums of money arising from a given annual saving employed in an assurance, and invested so as to accumulate at compound interest. I shall suppose the assurance to be made at the Equitable, and shall take the bonus added to each 100*l*., reckoning back from the year 1820, and assuming that the future additions will equal the past.

A person aged thirty-five might, by paying 100*l*. annually, assure 3343*l*.; and if his age were forty-five, the same sum would assure 2567*l*.

The sums to which persons of these ages would respectively become entitled at the Equitable Society, after any number of years, may be found very nearly by taking $\frac{21}{26}$ or $\frac{16}{26}$ of the sum in the second column, opposite the given number of years mentioned in the first.

Will possess at end of years.	A person aged twenty-five paying 100*l.* a-year premium, assures 4160*l.*	A person laying out 100*l.* a-year at three per cent.	Ditto four per cent.	Ditto five per cent.	Ditto six per cent.
10	5096	1146	1201	1257	1318
15	6032	1860	2002	2158	2328
20	7072	2687	2978	3307	3679
25	8528	3646	4165	4773	5486
30	10400	4757	5608	6644	7906
35	12688	6046	7365	9032	11143
40	15246	7540	9503	12080	15476
45	18054	9272	12103	15970	21274
50	20862	11280	15267	20935	29034
*55	23670	13607	19116	27271	39417
60	26478	16305	23799	35358	53313
65	29286	19433	29497	45680	71908
70	32094	23059	36429	58853	96793

The first remark which the inspection of this table suggests, is, that although the calculations of the premiums at the Equitable are made at three per cent., it is evident that that office could not have made the large additions which it has to all its policies, unless the rate at which it

* These four numbers are conjectural, supposing the additions to increase at the same rate as the last.

had improved its money were much higher.

If the interest of money were four per cent., a person aged twenty-five must live about sixty-five years, or reach the age of ninety, before he will have paid to the office a sum equal to that which he is to receive at his death. If money can be improved at five per cent., he must live nearly fifty years, and even at six per cent. he must live almost forty years, before the accumulations from his annual premiums amount to the sum he receives at his death. Now, according to the Carlisle tables, it is an even chance that a man aged twenty-five will live forty years; and the experience of the Equitable Society gives nearly the same result.

If the assurance is on a life of thirty-five, it must continue to exist above fifty years, when money produces four per cent., thirty-seven years if five per cent., and thirty years if six per cent. Now, the number of years which a life of that age has an even chance of reaching, is, both by the Carlisle and the Equitable tables, about thirty-three years.

If the assurance had been on a life aged

forty-five, he must have lived thirty-nine, twenty-eight, or twenty-three years, in order to have paid the office as much as he receives at his death; supposing the money to be improved at the respective rate of four, five, or six per cent. Now, a person aged forty-five has an even chance of living twenty-five or twenty-six years, by the Carlisle and Equitable tables.

From these tables the folly of assuring at any of the offices, where no additions are made to the policies, and where the same or nearly the same rate of premium is charged, is perfectly apparent; and it would also appear, from what has been stated, that if the same additions were to be made in future, which have during the last fifty years been added to policies at the Equitable, then, even as a method of saving, it would be highly advantageous to assure at that, or at a similarly constituted office: and this would be rendered still more advisable, when the slow rate at which money can now accumulate, arising from the low rate of interest, is taken into the consideration.

It would not, however, be reasonable to

presume that the same sums can be added continually for a long term of years, because, as has already been observed, there are causes in operation which will naturally diminish what may be called the mercantile profits of that institution ; and they will receive a considerable check from the great reduction in the interest of money, should it remain at its present rate for several years longer.

It is said, however, that they possess a large undivided capital, of which the public, from want of sufficient information, have very vague, and perhaps extravagant ideas. The legitimate use of such a capital is to equalize the fluctuations amongst the various circumstances on which the system depends ; and it would be wise to allow some portion of that capital to be absorbed during the time in which interest is unusually low, as it has been created when it was unusually high. This seems the only way to prevent a retardation in the profits, which the present rate of interest must, if of long continuance, at some future period, inevitably produce.

Having stated the nature of the different societies for assuring, some reasoning relative to the necessity of raising a large capital at the commencement, and the reasons which induce people to make assurances on lives, I shall now proceed to consider, in succession, the various circumstances on which the assurer should found his judgment in selecting the office to which he applies. Several of these particulars, although very essential to the soundness of his conclusions, are alluded to with much reserve, or altogether omitted in the prospectus which is given to the public by many of the offices; and some of these productions would appear, from their composition, rather to be addressed to those thoughtless people whose credulity is periodically duped by the splendid promises of the lottery, than to a class whose forethought and prudence are so decidedly evinced by the very circumstance of their desire to provide against the uncertainty of life. At the conclusion of this examination, I shall offer those reflections which appear to me to result from it.

CHAPTER IV.

Of Capital.

This usually occupies a prominent situation in the invitation to assurers, and is of very different extent at different offices. The following list is arranged according to the amount of subscribed capital at the respective offices :—

	£.	£.
Alliance	5,000,000	2,500,000
Rock	2,000,000	2,000,000
Guardian	2,000,000	1,000,000
Palladium	2,000,000	1,000,000
Crown	1,500,000	1,500,000
Atlas	1,200,000	600,000
British Commercial	1,000,000	1,000,000
European	1,000,000	1,000,000
Law Life	1,000,000	1,000,000
Albion	1,000,000	500,000
Hope	1,000,000	500,000
Globe	1,000,000	500,000
Eagle	1,000,000	500,000
Imperial	750,000	750,000
Royal Exchange	745,000	248,333
University	600,000	600,000
West of England	600,000	300,000
Union	300,000	150,000
Provident	250,000	250,000
Economic	200,000	200,000
Medico-Clerical		

In the second column I have reduced the capital of those offices which insure property against fire to one-half; and those which add to this business that of insuring ships, I have reduced to one-third. A few of the offices, as the London Assurance, the United Empire, and the Westminster, have not deemed it necessary to state the amount of their capital, amongst the explanation of the terms offered to the public; and several others on the plan of mutual assurance, as the Equitable, the Amicable, the London Life Association, the Norwich Union, have no subscribed capital.

It will be seen from this table, that above sixteen millions are pledged to the public for the fulfilment of contracts relative to lives. The greater part of this capital is, however, nominal, few of the societies having raised the whole amount subscribed. The following table, arranged according to the amount actually paid up, exhibits rather a different order from the preceding one. The same deductions have been made from the capitals of those offices which insure houses or ships.

	£.	£.
Globe	1,000,000	500,000
Alliance	500,000	256,000
Rock	200,000	200,000
Guardian	200,000	100,000
Atlas	120,000	60,000
Crown	150,000	150,000
British Commercial	100,000	100,000
European	100,000	100,000
Law Life	100,000	100,000
Albion	100,000	50,000
Hope	100,000	50,000
Eagle	100,000	50,000
Palladium	80,000	40,000
Imperial	75,000	75,000
University	60,000	60,000
Economic	50,000	50,000
Provident	25,000	25,000
Medico-Clerical		

The money actually paid up amounts to nearly two millions, or somewhat more than ten per cent. on the nominal capital.

Of these offices, the Globe is the only one in which the whole subscribed capital has been paid up; and as this office was established in 1803, probably the capital, thus raised, was invested in the funds nearly at that period. The price of three per cents * varied during that year from seventy-two to fifty, so that if the capital was invested at the lowest price, and were now converted into money, it would be nearly doubled.

* Highest price of three per cent. consols, February, 1803, 71$\frac{7}{8}$; lowest price of ditto, July, 1803, 50$\frac{1}{4}$.

CHAPTER V.

Of the Directors.

The government of the various assurance companies is vested in a certain number of directors, who are chosen by the proprietors, and are possessed of a certain quantity of stock, or are assured to a certain amount. The number of these directors varies from twelve to twenty-five. In those societies which are established solely for the purpose of dealing in these kinds of securities, and which do not profess to make *any return* of the profits, it is immaterial to the public in what manner their profits are shared amongst the partners, or how their officers and directors are paid: if they are paid too highly, the proprietors will receive a less dividend on their shares; but the public have no right to inquire into the subject, which is entirely a matter of arrangement amonst the partners: nor is such a knowledge of any value to the public in enabling them to judge whether the companies fulfil the contracts they have entered into. If the specific sum assured is punctually paid on the death of the nominee, without any vexatious difficulties being raised, full proof has been given of the just fulfilment of the original contract between the parties.

The case is, however, widely different with those companies which stipulate to return to the assured a given portion of the profits. It is a maxim, which might with advantage be more universally adhered to, that a man should not merely fulfil the engagements into which he has entered, but that he should also, if he possesses evidence which will demonstrate it, allow an examination of that evidence to those with whom he may have had dealings.* It is this principle which, by

* One of the regulations of the Palladium is, that "the whole of the accounts are to be regularly audited upon an improved and most efficient plan, and the *results thereof, without any reservation,* are to be sub-

giving publicity to the mode in which the large sums of money raised in this country for charitable purposes are expended, has produced an amount, that is justly an object of admiration amongst foreigners and of pride to ourselves.

If a company propose to give one-half (or any definite portion) of the profits of the establishment to those who are assured with it; in order to judge whether it has fulfilled its promise, it is necessary to know what those profits are, how they are estimated, how divided among the assured, and that the expenditure in conducting its business is not wasteful and extravagant. As (at present) only the influence of the expenditure on the interests of the public is the object of consideration, I shall illustrate its effects by an instance, which is, perhaps, not widely different from some that have occurred.

Suppose twenty-four persons subscribe

mitted to a general meeting annually, or oftener, if required." This deserves imitation; and, if rigidly adhered to, is the best security any society can offer to the public.

each 5000*l.* to form a capital of 120,000*l.*,* they might appoint themselves directors, and offer to return to the public half the profits; let us further suppose, that, after paying each of the directors 100*l.* a-year, and defraying all the other expenses of the establishment, the annual profits were to be 12,000*l.*; half this, or 6000*l.*, would be divided amongst the assurers, according to the agreement; but the spirit of that agreement might be easily defeated, although its letter would be adhered to by a little difference in the arrangement, whilst the reason of the apparent diminution in the profits could not be known to those who were not permitted access to the books of the society.

As the case has been at present stated, each subscriber of 5000*l.* would receive annually

As a director	100
As a shareholder at five per cent. .	250
Total .	£350

* This might represent a nominal capital of 1,200,000*l.*

But the proprietors, having the sole government, might resolve that the pay of the directors was insufficient, and might allow them an addition of 200*l.* each annually. This 4800*l.*, paid out of the income, will reduce the nominal profits to 7200*l.*; one-half of which (3600*l.*) goes to the public, and the other half will allow a dividend of three per cent. on the capital. In this case each subscriber of 5000*l.* would receive annually

As a director	300
As a shareholder	150
Total .	£450

If the public were unacquainted with the internal arrangement, by which the share of the profits assigned to them had been reduced from 6000*l.* to 3600*l.*, they might be induced to acquiesce in it, from considering that the proprietors also had suffered with them, by having their interest reduced from five to three per cent., whilst, in fact, those proprietors had each increased their incomes by 100*l.* a-year.

An additional allowance to directors might diminish the profits to any extent;

but it is manifest that a proceeding of this nature is quite contrary to the spirit of the promise held out to the public, and that if they are kept in ignorance of the rules and of the expenditure of the company, they have no check against the introduction of such abuses, nor any security that the promise is honourably fulfilled.

Having thus shown that the knowledge of the number, and payment of the directors, is by no means a matter of indifference to those who assure at an office which makes any return of a definite part of the profits, it should be observed, that this reasoning does not apply so forcibly to those in which the portion returned depends on the decision of the directors. In this case, the party assuring has agreed to purchase a policy, together with as much or as little of the profits as the directors may think fit to allot; and, however small that portion may be, he has, in strictness, no ground of complaint against the directors, but ought rather to blame his own folly in trusting to such a security. The salary of the directors of different offices is very various; at some being small, and at others very considerable: the manner in which it is paid also differs; in some it is only paid to those actually attending, in others it is an annual sum; and the situation has occasionally been held by a resident at a distance, thus converting it into a sinecure. That a large payment to the directors is not always necessary to the security and prosperity of such an institution, seems apparent from the circumstance, that in the largest society (the Equitable) the payment to each director is but small, and depends on the punctuality of his attendance. At the first institution, a sum, not exceeding forty shillings, was ordered to be divided at each court amongst the directors then present. In the year 1793, a new regulation was made, by which each director receives one guinea for every meeting of the directors which he attends.

At the London Life Association, no remuneration was allowed to the directors until a profit had been declared; it was then fixed at half-a-guinea each, a sum which was afterwards increased to one guinea.

The readiness with which gentlemen, of respectability, wealth, and intelligence, allow their names to be attached to companies, with whose principles they are but little acquainted, is much to be regretted. The public have been accustomed, and with some degree of reason, to infer the respectability of an undertaking from that of the names under whose sanction it is introduced, and to trust that the facts, stated in the prospectus, have been examined into, and are vouched for by the officers of the society.

The recent practices which have prevailed, of presidents, vice-presidents, and directors selling out their shares as soon as they reached a premium, and deserting those societies into which the public were alone induced to enter on the faith of their names; or, in some instances, the scarcely less reprehensible system of lending their names, without taking any share or interest in the concerns, have done much to remove this impression; to diminish the value justly attached to character and rank; and to reduce to one uniform level the artful projects of the designing adventurer, and the more prudent undertakings of forethought and calculation.

These observations apply chiefly to the numberless companies, whose names it is now needless to preserve. Fortunately, the subject of life assurance was too uniform in its results to attract the attention of many of those who instituted companies for the purpose of gambling in their shares, and in consequence, it partially escaped them.

There are, however, even amongst these institutions, some trifling inconsistencies, which it might be desirable to remove, or prudent to conceal.

For instance, an office holding out, amongst its advantages, the peculiarly high honour and integrity of its directors, should not pay a commission to the agents of other persons.

Nor should a society, partly "clerical," publicly hold out the same inducement.

It might be thought that a society, which takes "science exclusively for its guide," would scarcely select for the basis of its computation, one of the most incorrect of existing tables.*

Nor should we expect that the combined intellect of our two venerable seats of learning should, in the prospectus of their society, state a train of arithmetical reasoning, refuted by the data on which it is founded.† This latter is, however, a very venial error; nor should the public judge too severely of that simplicity which, whilst it gives the reasoning,

* The Northampton tables are, of any which possess the slightest reputation, those least calculated to represent the probable rate of mortality amongst a body of assurers; they are tables which an experience of thirty years has proved to be (for this purpose) erroneous throughout a large part, in the proportion of two to one.

† The following is an extract from the arguments advanced in the prospectus of the University Life Assurance Society:—

"In order to show the profits likely to result from assuring the lives of members of the Universities, it may be observed, that in the University Club, which consists of one thousand members, many of whom are not such lives as would be deemed insurable, only thirty-eight have died in three years; and, if the average be taken at the age of thirty-five, which, indeed, is too low, the deaths will be found much fewer than the ordinary rate of mortality, as shown by the best tables, would pro-candidly exposes the facts which overthrow it.

It is not to be inferred from these remarks, that the directors of the first of the four offices, above alluded to, are deficient in integrity, nor those of the second in morality. Those of the Palladium may not have mistaken the "infancy of science for its maturity;" nor are we to suppose the University incapable of reasoning logically.

duce." What table may be alluded to as the best, is, perhaps, difficult to determine. The following comparisons may throw some light on the subject:—

Out of one thousand persons, aged thirty-five, there die in three years

38 by the University Club experience.
33·1 by De Parcieux's table.
36·1 by Swedish tables, formed from twenty years, ending in 1795, males alone.
34·7 by the same, males and females.
30·2 by Swedish table, formed from five years, ending in 1805.
31·3 by the Carlisle tables.
33·2 by Equitable experience.

Out of these the Swedish, which are founded on the most numerous collection of facts, and the Equitable experience, which is the best adapted for determining the affairs of an office, show, that the mortality amongst the members of universities is rather high.

The conclusion, alike applicable to all, is, that such inconsistencies could only have arisen from the directors conceiving themselves relieved from all responsibility, with regard to the practices or statements of their offices.

CHAPTER VI.

Of the Rates of Premiums.

THE first question which usually arises, when a person proposes to assure his life, is, at what rate of premium can the assurance be effected? on this circumstance chiefly depends the amount he can secure to his executors.

It is, however, a great mistake to imagine that this is the only, or even the principal ground of determining the choice of the office to which the assurer should have recourse; there are other circumstances, of at least equal importance, which will be considered in succession. In Table III., the rates of all the offices for an assurance of 100*l.*, on the whole duration of a healthy life, are given, and to these are added two columns marked EE and EE thirty per cent.

The first of these has been calculated with care, from the comparison of the comparative decrements of the lives assured at the Equitable office, with the decrements at similar ages in the Northampton tables. As those decrements are only given for periods of ten years, they were divided into periods of five, in proportion to the similar decrements in the Northampton tables; and thus a kind of guide was established for the intermediate years: this, however, was not rigidly adhered to, and similar comparisons were instituted, in the latter part, with De Parcieux's and the Carlisle observations: the rate of interest adopted has been three per cent.

The difficulties of forming a table out of such distant observations, are known to those conversant with the subject, and their value must, in some measure, depend on the experience of the calculator.

The column marked EE thirty per cent., is formed by the addition of thirty per cent. to the former. From the first of these tables the reader will be enabled to see, at any age, what is the fair price of an assurance of 100*l*. on a life of that age, supposing no expense be incurred by the establishment, nor any profit be allowed; it is, in fact, a just equivalent for the risk, and is calculated from the best data which have yet been made known to the public. All that is charged beyond this sum must be regarded as charged for the expense of conducting the business of the offices, for the profit of proprietors, in a proprietary company, or for the security of the assurers, in a society on the principle of mutual assurance. The second of these columns, which does not differ very widely from several of the offices, shows the price which ought to be charged so as to allow of a gross profit of thirty per cent.

In order to facilitate the calculation of other contingencies dependent on life, I have computed two tables from the same data, and arranged them on the plan first pointed out by the late Mr. Barrett, whose laborious and extensive computations met with such little encouragement from the public.* The multitude of questions, to which this arrangement affords an easy solution, is very considerable; and in order to render them more useful, I have added the logarithms of the numbers, and in the Appendix have given a few of the algebraic solutions of the questions of most frequent occurrence. As the rate of interest which is produced by capital, is at present unusually low, it may be interesting to know the value of such contingencies, supposing two and a half per cent. to be the rate of interest; with this view, a table on the same principle of arrangement, and deduced from the same data, but adapted to an annual interest of two and a half per cent., is given.

The remarkable approximation of the Carlisle tables to those resulting from the

* Mr. Bailey, in an appendix to his treatise on annuities and life assurances, gave an account of the greater part of these enormous calculations, and endeavoured to promote the publication of a portion of them by subscription. I have been for some time in the possession of those alluded to, as well as others of much interest by the same unwearied calculator, but it is not probable that they would ever repay the great expense of printing.

Equitable experience, has already been pointed out by Mr. Milne,* whose observations on the materials and construction of tables have formed a valuable addition to our knowledge of this subject.

Although I do not feel satisfied that those tables represent the law of mortality amongst a great and indiscriminate population, yet from their near agreement with the largest experience of a select class, of which we have as yet any record, they will be adopted by some as the basis of their calculations. For this reason, as well as for the satisfaction of those who may desire to compare their results in any cases with those deduced from the Equitable experience, I have added a table on Mr. Barrett's principle, deduced from the Carlisle observations at three per cent.

As a further assistance in instituting any comparisons, a table is given of the values of an annuity on lives of all ages, as deduced from the Swedish observations computed by Dr. Price; from De Parcieux's observations computed by the late

* Supp. to the Encyclopædia Britannica, Mortality, art. 80, &c.

Mr. Maseres; from the Carlisle observations and the Equitable experience, both calculated by myself.

As most of the tables of rates differ at different ages, in a greater or less degree, from that deduced from the Equitable experience, in order to determine the rate of profit of the several offices, it is desirable to know the average age of persons who make assurances. From a table given by Mr. Morgan at the end of his work on assurances, we have, for every interval of ten years of life, the number of persons assuring at the Equitable. As this table is formed from above one hundred and fifty thousand instances, the conclusions to which it leads will probably be very near the truth. From this I have deduced the number forty-seven as the average age at which persons assure; that is to say, as many persons assure later in life than this period as at a younger age. It appears from this table that the largest number of assurers (not quite one-third of the whole) commence between forty and fifty years of age; that about nine-tenths of those who assure begin between the ages of thirty and seventy; and that not one-fifteenth part of the total number are under twenty when they commence.

The following table exhibits the profit per cent. on the premiums of the several offices, on an assurance on a life aged forty-six, which is about one year less than the average age of persons assuring:—

Alliance	30·2
Amicable	25·5
British Commercial	16·6
Crown	25·5
Economic	16·2
Equitable	29·8
European	21·5
Guardian	25·1
London Assurance	26·7
Medico-Clerical	29·7
Norwich Union	19·3
Sun	30·9
United Empire	21·9
University	23·2
West of England	16·9

The highest rates of profit are those of the Alliance and the Sun, which are a little more than thirty per cent., whilst the lowest are those of the British Commercial and the Economic, which are rather more than one-half the former, or a little above sixteen per cent. This table alone would form a very insufficient ground of judgment, and should always be viewed in conjunction with the proportion of profits returned to the assured, which will be discussed in another chapter. Thus, although the rate of profit taken by the Alliance and the Sun are the same nominally, since the former of these companies makes a return in the form of a bonus, the real profit ultimately paid by the assured may be considerably less in one than in the other : a similar remark applies to the other two offices just mentioned. It is worthy of observation, that the table of rates formed from the Equitable experience, by the addition of thirty per cent., agrees very nearly with the rates actually taken by that office at the average age of assuring life ; for all ages above forty-six, the sum required by that society is less, and for those which are younger than forty-six, it is larger. I think, therefore, that it may be fairly stated, that those offices which calculate their premiums by the Northampton tables make a gross profit of thirty per cent., without including the large additional profit that arises from the average rate of interest being above three per cent., the rate at which those tables are computed.

There are sixteen offices that adopt these rates, six of which do not make any return to the assured beyond the amount of the policy.

Names of the offices using the Northampton tables :—

Atlas.
Imperial.
Law Life.
London Life Association for persons not members.
Palladium.
Provident.
Rock.
Union.
Albion
Eagle.
Exchange Royal.
Globe.
Pelican.
Westminster.

The last six make no return beyond the amount of the policy.

It is difficult to say from what tables of mortality the premiums of many of the offices are calculated Those which adopt the Equitable rates use the Northampton tables; the Alliance and the Sun are guided to a certain extent by the Carlisle; but many offices seem to have arbitrarily altered those of the Equitable, according to their own fancy. For several of these it would be difficult to find any table of mortality which should represent their premiums; but the University Assurance Society stand unrivalled in their ingenuity, and have succeeded in manufacturing tables which it is impossible to derive from any rates of mortality, real or imaginary.

In order to render this intelligible to those who are not conversant with algebraical investigations, it may be observed, that when an office decides on any rate of premiums, payable during the whole life for the assurance of a certain sum on the death of the nominee, it is easy to compute from them a table of the values of annuities on lives of the same ages; and if the office wish to offer the public the option of compounding for these annual payments during life, by one payment at the commencement of the contract, or by a limited number of increased annual payments, it is not difficult to calculate from the tables of annuities so deduced, the fair equivalent for such payments; and when the tables of premiums are so formed, the office makes an equal profit whichever mode the convenience of the purchaser may induce him to adopt. Those who are not aware of the simple relation which exists between the values of assurances and annuities on lives of the same age,* are very liable to fall into the inconsistency, of calculating the tables of limited payments from a rate of mortality different from that by which they in reality computed the annual payments ; and such appears to have been the case with those whom the University Life Assurance Society employed to form their tables. The premiums deduced from the Northampton tables seem to have been altered for all ages up to fifty-seven ; and the value of the same assurance, to be paid for in five annual payments, has been calculated by the same tables without any alteration. Thus the public will at this

* The value of an annual payment (⊙ A) for an assurance of one pound is

$$= \frac{1}{1 + A} + v - 1,$$

where A is the value of an annuity on the same life, and v is the amount of one pound in one year at the same rate of interest.

Milne's *Treatise on Annuities*, vol. i. p. 336.

office pay more if they compound, than if they make annual payments.

That the public are beginning to inquire a little into the authority of the tables on which the premiums are computed, is apparent by the anxiety which several of the offices manifest to acquaint them that they possess new tables, although they rarely refer to any authentic data on which they are founded. This desire to be esteemed the possessors of some unpublished "standard," is curiously contrasted in the following paragraph, with an equal anxiety never to employ it.

"It has been the earliest wish of the "directors to obtain every possible ad- "vantage that could be derived from a "mathematical investigation of the exact "mean value of the duration of human "life; and they have accordingly deter- "mined on the adoption of a standard "table of annual mortality, which has "been deduced from a most extensive "comparison of documents, and has been "regulated and harmonized, by reducing "the result of experience to a symmetrical "form. This table is employed for the "determination of all such questions as "require extraordinary precision; but for "all the ordinary purposes of business it "has not been thought expedient to depart "from the general use of the tables almost "universally employed by other respecta- "ble offices."* Now the great mass, perhaps nine-tenths of the business of every office, consists in assurances for the whole term of life, paid for by annual payments; of the small remainder, the society have published tables applicable to all the ordinary cases. Of what consequence can it then be to the public, that in some rare case such superlatively refined means are to be employed? The directors might as reasonably have descanted to the public on the

* The directors of the Palladium appear to possess some curious "standard" dictionary as well as tables, in which the word "universally" has a novel meaning. In fact, about half the London offices do *not* use the Northampton tables.

It might, perhaps, contribute to the benefit of science, and certainly would assist the comprehension of the public, if the society would publish the data on which their tables are founded, and reserve their dictionary for the special use of the shareholders, with which arrangement, it is to be hoped, the latter would be more than "universally" contented.

" symmetry" of a statue concealed from all beholders, or on the " harmony" of a concert, from which they were to be carefully excluded.

CHAPTER VII.

Of the Proportion of Profits returned to the assured.

The high rate of the premiums demanded by societies for mutual assurance, whilst it gives security and permanence to those establishments is of comparatively little inconvenience to the public as from the division of the profits amongst the members, the money which they have contributed beyond the sum necessary for the risk and expense of management, is returned to them with its accumulations. In those societies where there is a large subscribed capital, such high premiums are unnecessary; and the public having begun to perceive the extravagant prices which they were paying, several of these societies, instead of reducing the cost of the commodity in which they dealt, have offered to give up to their customers a share of the profits of the business.

The general preference which they have manifested for this mode of adjusting their bargains, may arise from one or several of the following reasons.

The public may prefer the assurance of a sum which is to be augmented by a bonus to that of a fixed sum.

The companies may wish to meet the fluctuations, which a change in the rate of interest may temporarily produce, out of the sums allotted as additions rather than out of their own interest or capital.

The public, by having presented to them parts of a very complicated plan, of which it is impossible to judge without a knowledge of the rest, may be unable to discover the real profit which they are charged on all such transactions.

Ten of the offices are entirely proprietary companies, and do not make any return of profits; their names are as follows :—

Albion, N,	London Assurance,
British Commercial,	Pelican, N,
Eagle, N,	Sun,
Royal Exchange, N,	West of England,
Globe, N,	Westminster, N.

Those to which N is subjoined use the Northampton tables.

It is worthy of remark that seven of these ten require the highest price which is given for the assurance of lives, and one of them (the British Commercial) nearly the lowest.

The Equitable Society make periodic divisions, at intervals of ten years, of two-thirds of the profits, or of two-thirds of the excess of its assets above the demands to which it is liable; the remaining third forms part of the general stock, and continues to accumulate through the next ten years, until a new division again reduces the amount of their funds. The effect of this reserved third, as it relates to the assurer, is very different from that of an equal sum divided amongst a proprietary; in the latter case it acts as a continual drain on the profits of the assurer, whilst in the former it is constantly accumulating for his benefit. Supposing this third to amount to one million; at the end of ten years, at three per cent., it will have increased to 1,343,916*l.*; by two-thirds of which sum it augments the fund for division amongst the assured, so that they have an addition of 895,944*l.* more than if there had been a subscribed capital to divide the profits with them.

The Amicable Society used to divide seven-eighths of the annual payments of the members amongst those who die in the course of the year; but this arrangement having caused considerable inequalities, they have recently taken an average of five years; and, in order to secure a definite sum to the assured, they guarantee the product of each share to be not less than 200*l.*

The following table exhibits the proportion of profits returned to the assured by various offices:—

Amicable, seven-eighths.
Crown, two-thirds.
Economic, three-fourths, after deducting five per cent., on 50,000*l.*, or 2500*l.* annually.
Equitable, two-thirds.
Imperial, two-thirds.
Law Life, four-fifths.
London Life, one-fifth annually.
Medico-Clerical, a proportional part after paying the proprietors from three to five per cent.
Norwich Union.
Palladium, four-fifths.
Rock, nominally two-thirds after deducting 5000*l.*
United Empire, two-fifths, if the directors think fit.

University, four-fifths ; interest at five per cent. being first paid to the shareholders.
Alliance, unknown.
Atlas, unknown.
European, unknown.
Guardian,* unknown.
Hope, unknown.
Union, unknown.
Provident, share with the proprietors according to their respective contributions.

The reader may perhaps imagine that this table will enable him to form a correct judgment of the relative advantages of different offices ; but without a further inquiry than that of the mere proportional part of the profits returned, he will possibly arrive at a very erroneous conclusion. Six of the companies have not thought it necessary to inform the public what part of the profits they are to receive back ; and the few reasons which I have heard assigned for refusing this important information, are somewhat singular.† It is

* Limited by deed.

† Some of the companies promise to return portions of the profits which they do not specify, and one of them refuses the information, although it is stated to be determined by their deed. What is the reason for thus concealing from the public a fact with which it is essential for them to be acquainted, in order to judge of the fairness of the terms offered to them ?

said that when an office proposes to return a specific portion of its profits, a new one may arise which will undersell it, by offering a still larger share; this is evidently a benefit to the public. It is also asserted, that the share which some of the offices contract to return, although nominally one-half or two-thirds, is, in truth, from the manner of apportioning it, perhaps not one-quarter part of the profits; and that the public form an erroneous opinion from the proportions offered by different offices. This objection, although true in some instances, is not to be obviated by withholding the information, on which alone a correct judgment can be founded; and the fair way of meeting it is, to acquaint the public with the share to which they are to be entitled, and also the manner in which it is to be apportioned.

The only two companies which have yet assigned a bonus to the assured, by adding a certain per centage to the policies, are the Equitable and the Rock: the latter, in the year 1819, made its first septennial dividend of profits, and added at the rate of twenty per cent. to those policies which had existed ten years. These are therefore the only two offices between which, on this point, we can directly institute a comparison.

On referring to the statement of the sums added to policies at the Equitable Society, in different periods of ten years each, it will be found that

In the ten years ending in	Each policy had an addition per cent. of £	s.	d.
1782	15	0	0
1786	19	0	0
1791	14	0	0
1792	32	0	0
1795	30	0	0
1800	30	0	0
1810	22	10	0
1820	22	10	0

In ten years ending	The Rock added to each policy per cent. £	s.	d.
1819	20	0	0

The average addition at the Equitable, for a period of ten years, appears from this table to be 23*l*. 2*s*. 6*d*. per cent.

The decrease in the profits of the Equitable at the two latter decennial divisions, seems to have arisen from a larger portion than one-third of the profits having been reserved. This conjecture is corroborated by the large surplus which it is alleged is accumulated by that society.

A difference of 3*l.* 2*s.* 6*d.* on 20*l.*, or nearly one-sixth between two offices, may not appear very great; and it may perhaps be expected that on a larger experience they will approximate much more nearly to each other. That there are very sufficient reasons why this cannot be the case, and that the relative advantages of the two offices are not truly estimated by the numbers 20, and $23\frac{1}{8}$, I shall now proceed to show. In order to render this matter, which is of considerable importance, more clear, I shall suppose two assurance offices to commence at the same time, one on the plan of the Equitable, the other on that of the Rock and some others; that each makes by its business a clear profit of 300,000*l.* every ten years; each office awards two-thirds of the profits to the assured, but one of them, immediately on each division, transfers one-third of the profits to a body of proprietors.

By tracing the progress of these offices through a considerable period of years, we shall see the important result produced by the deduction of one-third of the profits for the payment of those who guarantee the capital.

At the end of the first ten years, both offices divide a profit of 300,000*l*., and two-thirds of this are added to the policies of the assurers at both offices; but at the Equitable, the other third increased during the next ten years, suppose it only at three per cent., amounts to 134,392*l*.; and at the second division, the profits of the Equitable are greater than those of the other office by this sum.

The following table will show the sums added, at intervals of ten years, by an office on the plan of the Equitable:—

	£.
At end of first ten years	200,000
——— second do.	289,595
——— third do.	329,730
——— fourth do.	347,709
——— fifth do.	355,764
——— sixth do.	359,373

Whilst at an office in which one-third of the profit is paid to proprietors, the constant sum of 200,000*l*. can only be added at the decennial period of division; and in the course of sixty years, the assurers have received additions of near 682,000*l.* at one office above those given by the others.

Nor is this the whole difference; for although two-thirds is the sum nominally divided amongst the assured, since that sum is only payable on the death of their respective nominees, it is not really equal to two-thirds, and is, in fact, different for different ages. Thus suppose three assurers of the ages of twenty, thirty-five, and sixty, and that 100*l.* is the addition awarded to each of their policies, the present value of that sum to each of these parties is 34*l.* 9*s.* 9*d.*, 42*l.* 3*s.* 1*d.*, and 61*l.* 7*s.* 9*d.** respectively; and even when the same sum is added to a policy on a life aged eighty, it is worth in present money only 82*l.* 2*s.* 10*d.*: this inequitable mode of apportioning them is not however so disadvantageous in a system of mutual assurers, because the reserved surplus

* These are the values allowed by the Equitable for each 100*l.* addition to their policies at these respective ages. The values by the Northampton tables at three per cent., 42*l.* 16*s.*, 50*l.* 13*s.* 4*d.*, 61*l.* 7*s.* 9*d.*, and 86*l.* 1*s.* 5*d.*

again accumulates for the benefit of the assured at the next period of division.

These facts show that the two-thirds, apparently given to the assured, are in reality not equal to one-half the total profits ; at the same time they explain the cause of the large additions made at the Equitable, and show that it cannot be expected that any of an equal extent, can ever be made by any society burthened with a permanent proprietary.

The following table shows the sums added per cent. to policies of different dates, as decided at the Equitable Society, by various general courts, up to the year 1820. Total amount added to policies of

	£.	
10 years' date	25	per cent.
15 do. do.	50	do.
20 do. do.	77	do.
25 do. do.	113	do.
30 do. do.	161	do.
35 do. do.	217	do.
40 do. do.	280	do.
45 do do.	347	do.
50 do do.	401	do

CHAPTER VIII.

Of the Mode of assigning the Bonus to the Assured.

This subject is intimately connected with the preceding, and is equally essential to be known by those who propose assuring their lives. There are two circumstances respecting it in which the public are interested; the first question is, whether the portion of profits agreed to be divided among the assured, is actually so divided? the second is, whether the manner of distributing it amongst those who have a claim on it is fair and equitable?

With respect to the first of these questions, it has already appeared from the reasoning relative to two offices, the Equitable and the Rock, that two-thirds of the profits are not divided amongst the assured, as they are led to believe by the prospectus; and this is the case with all those societies which do not add a larger sum to the policies than the absolute amount of the profit, unless indeed they allow an interest on the bonus.

The following is a summary of the modes of apportioning the bonus, classed as far as the nature of the subject admits :—

Equitable, Rock, Provident, Union,	added to policies.
Alliance, Guardian,	added to policy or applied to diminish premium.
Norwich Union, Provident, United Empire,	added to policies in proportion to amount of premiums paid.
Economic, European,	added to policies and interest on bonus paid annually.
Atlas, Law Life,	a reversionary sum equal to present bonus added to policy.
London Life,	applied to diminish premium or paid immediately.
Amicable,	a sum equal to the average annual payment, received by the society during the last five years, divided amongst those who die in every year.
Palladium,	added to policies on the most equitable principles of division
Hope, Imperial,	unknown.

Those offices which merely add the bonus to the policy are wrong on both the grounds which interest the public. In the first place they appear to give as a bonus a larger proportion than they in reality do give, and they also distribute that bonus very unequally; the older lives having a much larger portion than the younger. In some cases, an old life will receive twice as much as a young one, and yet the same rate per cent. is awarded to each.

The former objection is not applicable to those offices which apply the bonus to diminish or extinguish the future annua payments, provided a fair commutation be made, but they are still open to the latter, unless the mode of distributing the bonus amongst the different persons assured, be just.

Two offices, the Economic and European, allow an annual interest on the bonus allotted, but this, although much less objectionable than that of the Equitable, the Rock, and some others, cannot be pronounced perfectly correct, without a knowledge of the manner in which the bonus is apportioned.

A reversionary sum to be added to the policy equal to the present value of the bonus, is distinctly promised by the Atlas and the Law Life Association: this removes one of the objections; but the other remains, unless we are informed how the share of the assured is divided amongst themselves. One other circumstance should also be considered in estimating the real proportion of profit given to the assured. After paying the expenses of management, and all the demands arising from deaths, the sum remaining is in reality the profit, and if the office engage to return to the assured one-half, this is the sum which ought to be divided; but many of the companies first pay out of this fund an interest of from three to five per cent., or perhaps more, on the capital subscribed by the proprietors, and then divide the remainder as profit, in equal portions between themselves and the assured. There is no objection to this, as well as to many other practices, when they are distinctly stated, except that, from their variety and the complexity they introduce, the public have more difficulty in understanding the merits of the different establishments. If two companies both offer to return one-half of the profits to the assured, and one of them has a capital of 200,000*l.*, although their profits may be the same, if one of the offices deduct out of them an interest for the shareholders before the division is made, the results to the assurers will be very different. Let the divisions of both offices be made septennially, and let them each amount in the gross to 100,000*l.* Then in the office which takes interest on its capital before division :—

	£.
Profit in seven years	100,000
Interest on 200,000*l.* capital, at five per cent. for seven years	70,000
Nominal profit remaining . .	£30,000
One-half for assurers	15,000
One-half added to interest for proprietors	85,000
Total profit	£100,000
If interest is not allowed, one-half of profit for assurers	50,000
One-half for proprietor	50,000
	£100,000

In one case the assurers will divide amongst them 15,000*l*., in the other they will share 50,000*l*., and yet the proportion allotted to them is nominally the same.

The following statements are extracted from the terms of the various companies, in order that the reader may form his own judgment upon them :—

ALLIANCE.

At the periods of participation of the company in the profits of its concerns, every policy for the whole term of life, which shall have paid five entire annual premiums, shall, if the allowance be made in reduction of annual premium, be entitled to such reduction from the original charge as shall then, and from time to time, be declared; but if the allowance be in addition to the amount assured, that addition shall also be continually declared from time to time.

Persons assuring their own lives have the option of declaring, at the time of effecting the assurance, whether they will participate in the profits by an addition to their policy, or by a reduction of premium.

ATLAS.

Persons assuring for the whole term of life for 100*l.* and upwards, in Great Britain and Ireland respectively, will be entitled, at the end of every seventh year, to participate in the surplus premiums, to be then ascertained by actual valuation.

ASYLUM.

The directors have power to divide such portion of the profits quinquennially as may not imprudently check the growth of the funds intended for the benefit of the assured.

CROWN.

Two-thirds of such profits as shall periodically be declared divisible, will be apportioned amongst assurers for the whole term of life, and may be applied to the reduction of the future annual premiums, or to the increase of the sum assured, as may be desired.

ECONOMIC.

A present three-fourths of the savings and profits divided amongst the assured entitled to participate therein, by additions to their policies, proportioned to their respective contributions, and in order to afford them the immediate benefit of such additions, interest thereon applied annually in reduction of their premiums.

EQUITABLE.

That in case any prospective addition shall hereafter be ordered to be made to the claims upon policies of assurance in this society, such order shall not take effect with respect to any policy granted after the 31st of December, 1816, until the assurances existing in the society prior in number and date to such policy, and if of the same date, prior in the number thereof, shall be reduced to five thousand; but as soon as such reduction shall have been ascertained, in manner hereinafter mentioned, the said policy shall be within the effect and operation of the order for such addition, as to the payments made thereon subsequent to such ascertained reduction: so that if such order should be made to take effect generally from the 1st of January, 1820, for the space of ten years then next following, a policy effected in the year 1817, shall not be within the operation of such order, until the assurances existing prior to the number and date of the policy, as aforesaid, shall have been reduced to five thousand; but such policy shall be within the operation thereof from the time when the reduction shall have been ascertained, in manner hereinafter mentioned, as to the payments made thereon subsequent to such ascertained reduction. And the like as to other cases. And this by-law shall be considered as a part of every such order, and shall be virtually incorporated therein, although the same may not be thereby expressly referred to.

That in case any retrospective addition shall hereafter be ordered to be made to claims upon policies of assurance in this society, such order shall not take effect with respect to any policy granted after the 31st of December, 1816, until the assurances existing in the society prior in number and date, and if of the same date, prior in the number thereof, shall be reduced to five thousand; but when the said reduction shall have been ascertained in manner hereinafter mentioned, such policy shall be within the effect and operation, and entitled to the benefit of such order, with respect to every payment made thereon subsequent to such ascertained reduction; so that if such order shall be made to take effect generally as to payments made before the 1st of January, 1820, a policy effected in the year 1817 shall not be within the effect and operation thereof, unless the life assured shall exist, and the payments continue to be made, until the assurances existing in the society prior to the number and date of the policy, as aforesaid, shall be reduced to five thousand; but as soon as such reduction shall have been ascertained, in manner hereinafter mentioned, such policy shall be within the effect and operation of such order for the several payments made thereon as aforesaid. And the like as to other cases. And this by-law shall be considered as a part of every such order, and be virtually incorporated therein, although the same may not be thereby expressly referred to.

That an inquiry be made on the 1st of

April in every year, in order to ascertain the number of assurances made and existing in the society; and when it shall have been ascertained by such inquiry that the assurances existing prior to the 1st of January, 1817, were, on the 31st of December immediately preceding such inquiry, reduced below the number of five thousand, the actuary do report the same to the court of directors, who shall communicate such report to the quarterly general court, to be holden in the June following; and that as many of such policies as had been made subsequent to the 31st of December, 1816, and which were existing in the society on the 31st of December immediately preceding such inquiry, be added, according to the priority in their dates and numbers, and if of the same date, according to the priority in their numbers, to those above mentioned, as shall be sufficient to complete the number to five thousand; and that the persons holding the policies so added shall be considered thenceforward as entitled to such additions, as shall be thereafter made in respect of all the payments made subsequent to such ascertained reduction, and, under the same restrictions, to the same privileges of attending at the general courts, and of being eligible to the office of director.

That after the vacant numbers in the assurances existing in the society on the 1st of January, 1817, shall have been filled up agreeably to the foregoing order, the actuary on the 1st of April in every succeeding year do ascertain the vacancies which have taken place in the preceding year in the policies constituting the five thousand mentioned in the fifth resolution, and report the same to the court of directors, who shall communicate such report to the quarterly general court in the month of June following; and that as many policies shall be added, according to the priority of their dates and numbers, and if of the same date, according to the priority in their numbers, as shall be sufficient to complete the number to five thousand: and that the persons holding those policies shall thenceforward be considered as entitled to such additions as shall be thereafter made in respect of all payments made subsequent to the 31st of the preceding December, and, under the same restrictions, to the same privileges of attending the general courts, and being eligible to the office of director.

Provided that nothing hereby ordered shall be construed to authorize an addition to the sum assured by any policy, upon which policy the number of payments required in that respect by the present by-laws of the society shall not have been made.

N.B.—Those by-laws require that six annual payments at the least shall have been made before any addition to a claim can take place ; and when such payments shall have been made, the party will be qualified to be received, in his turn, into the number of persons entitled to additions as aforesaid.

EUROPEAN.

The profits derived by this company are distributed amongst the several persons connected with the establishment, according to the contingency or certainty of their contract.

Life insurers derive an immediate benefit by the reduction of the premiums generally taken, with the prospect of a liberal addition to their policies, or a further reduction of the premium in ten years.

GUARDIAN.

Persons assured for the whole term of life will be entitled at the end of every seven years to participate in the profits of the company, after a deduction of such sum per annum, for the guarantee of the capital, as the directors may think reasonable, the extent of which is however limited by the deed of settlement.

The share of the profits to be so allowed to the assured, may either be added to the amount of their respective policies, or the value thereof be applied in reduction of the premiums hereafter to be payable on such policies, provided such option be declared in writing within three calendar months next after the dividend shall have been declared; but if such option be not declared, such share of profits will be added to the amount of policies.

HOPE.

Every person effecting a policy of assurance at this office, is entitled to a participation in the profits equally with the proprietors of the company, after a moderate deduction for the guarantee and the expenses of management.

IMPERIAL.

Upon every policy effected for the whole term of life, the assured will participate in the profits of the company, by having periodical additions made to the sums insured to the amount of two-third parts of such clear gains and profits.

LAW LIFE.

At stated periods, the surplus of the fund arising from the premiums of assurance, and their accumulation beyond what may be thought necessary to answer the expected claims upon the society, will be ascertained; and as large a portion of the savings as may be deemed consistent with the security of the institution, will be divided between the proprietors and the assured, in the following manner:—One-fifth will be transferred to the proprietors' guarantee fund, and reversionary sums, equivalent to the remaining four-fifths, will be added to the policies of those who shall have been three years assured for the whole term of life.

LONDON LIFE ASSOCIATION.

The distinguishing principle of this society is, that the benefits resulting from its transactions shall be enjoyed by the members during life, so as to render life assurance as easy to the assured, as a due regard to security will admit.

MEDICAL AND CLERICAL.

Persons assured for the whole term of life, will be entitled to share with the original proprietors the general profits of the business, in proportion to the amount of their respective assurances.

NORWICH UNION.

The whole of the surplus premiums is added at stated periods to the policies of the members, in proportion to the sums they have respectively contributed.

PALLADIUM.

A general investigation of the affairs of the society is to take place every seventh year, when four-fifths of the declared profit of the life department will be appropriated by way of bonus or addition, to be placed to the credit of the policies then in force for the whole term of life, upon the most equitable principles of division.

ROCK.

That the said bonus shall be short of the actual surplus profits at the time of making the same, by the sum of 5000*l.* at least.

That the bonus so declared shall be divided into three equal parts.

That one of the said parts shall be added to and consolidated with the subscription capital stock. (This is the proprietors' fund.)

That the remaining two-thirds be allotted to the policies in the manner described in the deed.

That the sum to which any person assured by the company may become entitled under any such distribution, shall be paid by the company without interest, at the time when the sum assured by the policy shall become payable, and not before.

UNION.

Those who assure with this company will participate with the proprietors in the profits of the establishment, which will be added every seven years to the respective policies.

UNITED EMPIRE.

Persons effecting assurances for the whole continuance of life, will at the end of the first five years, and of every subsequent five years, be entitled to participate in whatever net surplus profits it may be declared by the directors expedient to divide.

Two-fifths of the aforesaid profits will be divided amongst the said assured, in proportion to the premiums they may respectively have paid, and will, at their option, be either added to the amount of their policies, or applied in reduction of their future premiums.

UNIVERSITY.

As it is intended that the capital advanced shall be repaid to the shareholder, with a bonus of 100*l.* per cent., one-tenth of the profits, when ascertained by a valuation of all existing risks, will every five years be applied to form a fund for that purpose.

The remaining nine-tenths of the profits to be divided between the assured and the shareholder, in the proportion of eight parts to the former and one to the latter.

The profit or bonus to the assured to be given either by a diminution of the rate of premium, or by an increase of the amount of policy, at the option of the party.

CHAPTER IX.

Of the Periods of Division.

It is not usual with assurance offices to strike a balance annually, by which the state of their accounts may be accurately known; they generally, at stated intervals of five, seven, or ten years, balance their accounts, and at those times declare a profit or bonus amongst the assured. The reason assigned for these long intervals has been, the difficulty of the calculations on which such valuations are founded.

This difficulty has, I am inclined to believe, been considerably overrated; and, by the aid of an improved system of keeping the accounts, and tables properly adapted to the purpose, it would be by no means difficult to assign annually to each assurer his proportion of the profits which may have accrued during the past year.

Another reason which operates more than will perhaps be allowed, both in this and in other arrangements, is, that, by dividing the profits at distant intervals, a larger nominal sum is assigned to the assurers. It ought, however, to be remembered, that the assurer is not really benefited by this specious appearance; and that, whether the money given as a bonus accumulate in the hands of the society or in his own, its amount will at the stated periods be precisely the same.

It may be presumed that annual divisions of profit will be liable to fluctuate in their amount more considerably than those made at more distant intervals. This is likely to be the case, but the remedy is obvious; instead of determining the bonus by the profits of the preceding year alone, it may be made from an average of any given number of the preceding years: the larger this number, the more uniform its amount will be. This method has already been adopted by the Amicable Society, and may be considered as a valuable addition to their plan.

The following table shows the periods

at which divisions of profits take place at the respective offices :—

Amicable, London Life,	yearly.
Alliance, Asylum, United Empire,	five years.
Medical and Clerical,	five or seven years.
Atlas, European, Guardian, Norwich Union, Palladium, Rock, Provident, Union,	seven years.
Equitable,	ten years.
Crown, Economic, Hope, Imperial, Law Life,	unknown.

The distance between the periods at which the divisions of profits are made, is by no means an immaterial consideration in deciding on the office at which we should assure; the professed object of those divisions is to return part of the premiums, which it is admitted are greater than the risk requires. In a company of mutual assurers, it is quite right and prudent to take a considerable excess of premium, in order to prevent the fluctuations in the number of deaths rendering any call necessary. Although, if the premiums have been properly calculated, and the affairs of the society prudently conducted, such calls cannot fail in a few years to be repaid, and the society to flourish, yet they are likely to create alarm, and from that circumstance injure the credit of the society, and check its more extensive growth. But where there exists a subscribed capital, its very object is to equalize such variations, and it is unreasonable to demand as large premiums as are proper in a society of mutual assurance.

The whole object of assurances is, to render that certain which nature has made uncertain. A person in health and employment knows that if he lives a few years, he will be able to leave at his death a competence for his family; but he knows also that, from the uncertainty of life, he may be cut off in a year or in a month, and leave that family unprovided for: thus situated, he has recourse to an assurance on his life, and he is now certain of leaving a provision for his family.

It is this certainty with regard to pecuniary affairs, which it is the object of every prudent man to attain, that as it causes all assurances, so it ought to be our guide in arranging the plans by which they are effected. In accordance with this maxim, of rendering every thing certain which the nature of such institutions will admit, it is right that the periods for dividing the profits should be fixed, as well as that their occurrence should be frequent. The inconveniences arising from indefinite periods are, that the value of policies, subject to such additions, is less than if those periods were fixed; and that it is possible for those who may have a knowledge when such divisions are about to be made, to purchase at an insufficient price the policies of other persons, who may not possess the same information.

The periods of dividing the profits at the Equitable have varied at different times; they are, however, now fixed at intervals of ten years. This distance considerably diminishes their value: for if a person commence insuring at fifty-four, his chance of receiving a bonus at the first decennial division is about three-fourths, and his chance of gaining a second is nearly one-half. The greater the age of the assurer, the more injurious to his interest are such distant periods of divisions.

The tendency of long intervals between the times of declaring a bonus, is to cause too much to be paid to one class, by giving too little to another class of assurers; those who live longest will be the gainers, whilst those who are short-lived, or who die immediately before a division, will be the losers.

The system of a septennial division of profits, which is the one most generally adopted, is preferable to that of the Equitable Society, but is still inferior to a period of five years, whilst an annual division distributes the profits with more regularity and justice than any other. In such a system the nominal sums apportioned may not be so large, but the real advantage to the assured is more universally distributed. It would, however, be desirable to render these annual divisions more uniform in amount, by determining them from the average of a certain number of the preceding years: the first of these annual divisions, therefore, should not commence until after as many years have elapsed as the average is to be deduced from.

CHAPTER X.

Of the Periods at which Assurers become entitled to participate in a Division of Profits.

Most of the assurance companies which divide any part of their profits with the assured, do not allow the latter to participate in them, until they have paid a certain number of annual premiums. The number of payments which qualify is usually six: this is the number required at the Equitable. There exists, however, in that society a by-law but little known to the public,* which is contrary to the original spirit of its institution, and which has the effect of assimilating it, in

* The society print it, and distribute it in their book of terms; it appears to have been made with the view of reducing the number of assurers, which was at the time of its introduction rapidly increasing. As soon as it becomes sufficiently understood by the public at large, there is no doubt that it will fulfil those intentions.

in a greater degree than is generally imagined, to a proprietary company. As this has been already printed, the reader is requested to turn back from page 90 to 95.

The substance of these regulations may, I believe, be more briefly stated, thus :—

First.—That whenever any addition shall be made to claims on policies, it shall only take place upon the first five thousand policies in the society's books.

Secondly.—That in apportioning the bonus thus assigned to these five thousand, each policy shall be considered as having been opened on the day on which it was first declared to be within the limit of those five thousand.

Thirdly.—That these rules shall not alter that which makes it essential to have paid six annual payments before an addition can be made; and that, annually, certain means shall be resorted to to determine which are the five thousand first policies on the books of the society.

This law has made a marked difference between two large classes of the society, those who assured previous to 1817, and those who opened policies at that office at a later period. The former must for many years enjoy the profits contributed by the latter. In order to judge better of its effect, it will be necessary to know the number of persons assured for the whole term of life at the Equitable office. On inquiry the last autumn, (1824,) I was informed that there were about nine thousand. These are of course of a variety of different ages, but in order to form some judgment of the probable time it would require to reduce that number of persons, by deaths amongst them, to five thousand, I have drawn up the following table, supposing nine, eight, and seven thousand persons to be all of the same given age.

Each aged	Nine thousand, reduced by deaths to five thousand in	Eight thousand, reduced by deaths to five thousand in	Seven thousand, reduced by deaths to five thousand in
	years.	years.	years.
40	27½	23½	19
45	23½	20	17
50	20	17	13½
55	17	13½	11½
60	15	12½	9½
65	12	10	8
70	10	8½	6½

From this it will be seen that eight thousand persons, each aged fifty-five, will be reduced by deaths to five thousand in thirteen years and a half.

This is deduced from the table given in the Appendix as the result of the Equitable experience, which is the best adapted for the present purpose.

Now, supposing that as many deaths would happen amongst the assurers as if they were all aged fifty-five, then, if I had assured the life of the friend, at whose request I made the application alluded to, in all probability he would have been obliged to pay seventeen annual premiums, before he could be qualified, under these new regulations, to participate in the profits: this would happen in the year 1841, or just one year after the decennial division. He must, therefore, continue paying his annual premiums nine years longer, before that qualification could be of any avail; thus he would not, in truth, partake of the profits until twenty-six years after he began to assure. Now, unless a person be younger than the age of forty-four, even though he be such a life as the Equitable would admit, he has not an even chance of living twenty-six years.

The effect of these regulations will be beneficial to the interests of those who were assured prior to 1817, unless, when they become generally known, they should prevent the increase of the society, a result which they seem well calculated to accomplish. In the mean time, as no judgment can be formed by the public of the time at which they will probably share in the profits of that society, without a knowledge of the number of policies existing in its books, it is but reasonable to expect that that number should be annually published, and printed with the tables of terms distributed by the society.

An interval of ten years between the divisions of the profits of a society, combined with that regulation which allows those only to participate in them who have paid six annual premiums, is alone sufficient to postpone to a considerable distance of time any additions which can be made to the policies. If the first premium is paid in the fifth year, before a division of profits is to take place, then, as the sixth premium will be paid just after a decennial division, the assurer will not receive any addition to his policy until the expiration of fifteen years.

If he had commenced his payments one year sooner, he would have had his first bonus at the end of six years. A similar remark may be made respecting those offices which make septennial divisions : if they require the assured to have made five payments before he is entitled to a bonus, it is possible that he may insure at such a time as to receive no increase to his policy until the end of twelve years.

From the circumstances just alluded to, it may happen that two offices, whose terms are in general equally eligible, may present some difference from the nearness or remoteness of the time at which the profits are divided.

CHAPTER XI.

Of the Limits of Travelling allowed to the Assured.

By the conditions of the policies granted, all the offices restrict the assured to a residence within the limits of Europe, or require an additional premium (the magnitude of which varies according to circumstances) from those who travel into any other quarter of the globe. As the tables have been calculated from deaths amongst Europeans, some addition is perfectly just to pay for the greater risk which arises from a change of climate; it is however extremely desirable that tables of such additional risks for different ages, and various climates, should be published, as well as the observations on which they are founded. Wherever the true value of a risk is not ascertained by an enumeration of cases, the price of a guarantee against it is higher than it need be, and the variations in its price are larger.

I had occasion, a short time since, to inquire the price of assuring the life of a friend who had an intention of going to India, and I found the addition, charged for the risk from climate, to be at some offices nearly three times as great as at others: and the total charge at the most expensive office, was to that at the cheapest very nearly as eleven to six.

Most of the offices allow the assured to go by sea from one part of Great Britain to another without any additional premium; they however require, that the voyage shall be performed in decked vessels, king's packets, regular packets, or steam boats, some permitting one, some several, or all of these modes of conveyance. The islands of Guernsey, Jersey, Alderney, and Sark being included by a few of them

During peace, the assured are allowed to pass, in the vessels just named, from England to several ports in the channel; the most prevalent limits are between the Texel and Brest: these are admitted by the following offices :—

British Commercial,
Globe,
Guardian,
Hope,
Law Life,
London Assurance,
Provident,
West of England.

The following are the limits allowed by other offices :—

Alliance.—Texel and Havre.
Atlas.—Any ports in the channel.
European.—Elbe and Brest.
Imperial.—Ostend, Havre.
London Life.—Helvoet and Brest.
Norwich Union.—Elbe and Brest.
Sun.—Hamburgh and Bordeaux.
United Empire.—Any port of Europe to any other port.
Westminster.—Calais and Boulogne.
Pelican.—Only to and from Ireland in government packets.
Equitable.—Helvoet and Brest.

It is to be observed, that some of the offices have not restricted these voyages to times of peace. The Sun and the United Empire have allowed the widest limits ; and if the prices charged for the assurance of lives had not been such as to yield a very high rate of profit, it would have been quite reasonable to make an addition for some of the voyages, which are now allowed to be made without any further payment. The English Channel is by no means free from danger, whilst, in a voyage to Bordeaux, the waves of the bay of Biscay are almost proverbial; and the mouths of the Elbe are, perhaps, still more dangerous. Whenever, therefore, the present rates of assurance shall become considerably reduced, as in time they must, or whenever another mutual assurance society shall be instituted, it might be desirable to restrict the limits, perhaps to the Texel and Brest, and to charge a certain small addition for other more dangerous voyages: this addition should, however, be precisely stated in the terms distributed to the public by the office; for it can never be sufficiently insisted on that those terms should be as definite in all their parts as the nature of the subject will admit, and as little as possible should be left to the discretion of the directors.

CHAPTER XII.

Of the Deposits on proposing an Assurance

Several of the offices require of a person who proposes to effect an assurance, that he should leave a deposit according to the amount of the proposed sum: this deposit is returned if the company decline assuring the life which is offered, and is admitted as part of the first payment in case it should be accepted.

The reason that is assigned for this practice is, that it prevents applications where there is no intention of effecting a policy; surely, however, the number of such can be but few, and the trouble thus caused must be of very small amount.

There may perhaps be other reasons, but I am not aware of any very convincing ones in favour of the practice.

A person wishing to sell an annuity, may probably more readily meet with a purchaser, if he can at the same time offer an engagement from a respectable office to assure the life, on which the annuity depends, for a sum equal to the purchase money: and I should rather conceive that it would be an advantage to an office that this annuity should be sent to market with the offer of the company appended to it; because it would evidently have a tendency to induce the purchaser to give a preference to that office where the forms and trouble of application had already been passed through.

For the assurance of ordinary healthy lives, tables are published by all the offices, therefore the price is known before the life is proposed In extraordinary cases, as for example, where the party assured proposes to reside in a foreign climate, or to pursue some dangerous avocation, the terms can only be known by application at the office, and by their estimate of the risk of each particular case: to require a deposit in this case, would have the effect of preventing the assurer from acquiring a knowledge of the prices charged by different societies, which are often for such risks widely different, and it would thus check competition.

It is, therefore, desirable for the public that no such charge should be made; and it may be remarked, to the credit of several of those establishments which more particularly undertake extraordinary risks, that they scarcely ever require a deposit for information relative to the price.

The following are the deposits required by the several offices in proposing a life to be assured :—

	£.	s.	d.	
Alliance	0	5	0	if under 250*l*.
	0	2	0	above 250*l*.
Amicable	0	2	6	per cent.
British Commercial .	0	5	0	if under 100*l*.
	0	10	0	if under 500*l*.
	1	0	0	if under 1000*l*.
	1	0	0	for every additional 1000*l*.
Hope	0	2	6	per cent.
London Life Association	1	1	0	
Rock	0	5	0	if under 100*l*.
	0	10	6	if under 500*l*.
	1	1	0	if under 1000*l*.
Provident	0	2	6	per cent.
Law Life	1	1	0	

No deposit is required at the offices not mentioned in this table.

It is usual, when the risk which it is proposed to the office to undertake requires difficult calculations, as must sometimes happen, to ask for a deposit proportional to the time the computation occupies; and this deposit is not to be returned, in case the party proposing decline the terms offered by the company, but is to be considered as a payment for the labour which has been bestowed on the question.

Such a regulation is perfectly just; and without it, persons having no intention of dealing with the several companies might, by stating a case to them, acquire the opinions of the most skilful persons, without making them any remuneration for the time thus consumed.

CHAPTER XIII.

Of Entrance Money.

It is a practice pursued by a few of the assurance companies, to charge an additional sum on the first payment, which is usually called entrance money. This is generally appropriated to some particular fund, indicated in the deeds of the respective companies.

The following list comprises all those offices at which it is required, and also the amount :—

	s.	*d.*	
Amicable	10	0	per cent.
Equitable	5	0	per cent
London Life Association .	5	0	per cent.
Rock	5	0	per cent.

It may be remarked, that three out of the four offices which require this payment are established on the principle of mutual assurance.

The Rock, which is a mixed institution, is the only one containing a body of proprietors who have adopted this rule.

CHAPTER XIV.

Of Fines for Non-appearance.

It is required by all the companies, that the party on whose life an assurance is to be made, should appear personally at a meeting of the directors; but as this may be highly inconvenient to persons at a distance, it is generally dispensed with, on the payment of a certain sum per cent., estimated on the first payment only. It is perfectly reasonable that a fine for non-appearance should be required, because it in fact causes an additional risk: for even when the certificates required from the referees are quite satisfactory, it sometimes happens that a board of directors refuse to undertake the risk from some appearance of latent disease, which a medical eye may detect in the countenance or person, long before it becomes observable to others.

If this source of security to the company is given up, it is right to demand an equivalent in the shape of a fine.

I am not acquainted with any attempt to calculate the fair value of such additional risks, which, from the want of data, would possibly be accompanied with some difficulty; but I am induced to believe, that the sum of five shillings per cent., which is required by almost all the offices for the non-appearance of an assurer, for one year only, is greater than its true value for young lives, whilst it may be equal to or less than that value for older lives.

The table at the end of this work, containing the number of persons dying annually, according to the experience of the Equitable Society, may supply some means of judging, by instituting a comparison between it and a table of mortality formed from a more indiscriminate mixture of lives. This, however, would not be a true measure, because it is presumed that the lives proposed are in other respects eligible. A much more accurate estimate might be formed, if we possessed a table of the number of persons of various ages who have been rejected at the Equitable solely on the ground of their appearance, and if we could ascertain the duration of life of any considerable number of them: this latter condition is almost impossible; but the information which that society must possess would be, notwithstanding, a valuable addition to our knowledge.

Fortunately, the smallness of the risk renders our want of data to estimate it of no material consequence.

The following table exhibits the amount of fine for non-appearance, on assurances of various terms, required by different offices:—

Table of Fines for Non-appearance of an Assurer for the whole Term of Life.

Office	Per Cent.			Office	Per Cent.		
Albion	£0	15	0	London Assurance	£1	0	0
Alliance	1	0	0	London Life Association			
Amicable	0	10	0	Medico-Clerical			
Atlas	0	10	0	Palladium	1	0	0
British Commercial	1	0	0	Pelican	1	0	0
Crown				Provident	1	0	0
Eagle	0	15	0	Rock	0	15	0
Equitable	1	0	0	Sun	1	0	0
European				Union			
Exchange, Royal	1	0	0	United Empire			
Globe	0	15	0	University			
Guardian				Westminster	1	0	0
Hope	1	0	0	West of England	0	15	0
Imperial	1	0	0				
Law Life	1	0	0				

CHAPTER XV.

Of the Time allowed for the Payment of Premiums.

It may not be convenient to every person assured to pay his annual premium on the very day on which it becomes due, nor is it very material to the office, provided it be paid within a short time: the only inconvenience is the loss of the interest on the premium for a few days. There must, however, be some limit, beyond which, if the assurer neglect to pay his premium, the contract must be considered at an end, and the policy forfeited.

The following offices allow fifteen days:—

Albion,	London Assurance,
Atlas,	Palladium,
British Commercial,	Pelican,
Eagle,	Provident,
European,	Royal Exchange,
Globe,	Sun,
London Life Association,	Union.

The Hope allows twenty days.

The United Empire allows twenty-one days.

The following allow thirty days :—

Alliance,	Imperial,
Crown,	Law Life,
Equitable,	University,
Guardian,	Westminster.

The Amicable allows three months.

If the premium is not paid within the time limited, the forfeiture of the policy may still be prevented at most of the offices, by paying the premium, and also a fine, usually about one per cent. on the amount assured, and giving a warranty that the life assured is in good health.

CHAPTER XVI.

Of the Payment of the Sum assured on the Death of the Nominee.

On the death of any person whose life is assured, notice should be given to the office which has granted the policy, and all the required information and certificates should be forwarded as soon as possible. It is usual with most of the offices to pay the amount of the policy and profits which may have accrued at the end of three months after the death of the party has been established by sufficient proof. The Equitable and European require six months, and the Albion pays it in thirty days. At the United Empire one-fifth part of the sum, if under 200*l.*, is paid immediately, and the remainder in three months.

It is reasonable that some time should be suffered to elapse after the death of the party, to allow time for inquiries respecting the cause of death, or into any other circumstance which may require investigation; three months is not too long a period for this purpose, and is that which is most generally adopted. The plan of paying a portion immediately, which is pursued by the United Empire, must, in many cases, be a great advantage to the executors of the deceased, as it provides them with an immediate fund for the payment of expenses, which must be incurred before any other means can become available.

CHAPTER XVII.

Of Commission to Agents.

Few persons effect assurances on their lives without previously consulting either their solicitor, their agent, their broker, or some other person on whose judgment and integrity they imagine they can rely. It is therefore of the utmost consequence that no motive should be presented to those who are thus confidentially employed, which should induce them, from any prospect of advantage to themselves, to recommend one office in preference to others. That such a motive is constantly held out, and the temptation most frequently accepted, is established by too many proofs to be denied; and the frequency of its occurrence is unfortunately so great, as to cause it in some measure to have lost, in the eyes of those who practise it, the disgrace which, in all other transactions, is attached to the offer or the acceptance of a bribe.

In order to clear the way for the observations which will be offered on this subject, it is necessary to take a short view of the nature of an agent. An individual or a company exercising any trade, may employ a person to travel for them or reside permanently at any place, to procure orders; the persons so employed are known to those with whom they deal as agents, and of course any representations they may make of the merit of the goods they are employed to sell, are duly weighed by the purchasers as coming from persons acknowledged to be interested in the disposal of them. Whatever be the sum paid by the principal to his agent, is of little consequence to the consumer.

Let us now suppose the consumer, doubtful of his judgment, employs an agent of his own; it will never be contended that an individual or a body of men can, with any semblance either of justice or integrity, offer to those agents a premium to buy at their particular establishments the article they are instructed to purchase. If such a principle is once admitted, those who sell the worst goods will both find it necessary, and be able, to offer the highest premium for a breach of trust in the consumer's agent. Yet this is precisely the conduct of almost all the assurance companies: some of them unblushingly offer, even in the statement of their terms, and most of them privately pay, what they call a commission, to those persons who bring assurances to their office.

The following are extracted from some of the printed papers of terms:—

Albion.—A liberal commission is allowed to solicitors and others who effect life insurance.

Ditto.—A large commission is allowed to solicitors, brokers, and others, who effect life insurances.

British Commercial.—A liberal allowance is granted to solicitors and others recommending business to the office.

Eagle.—Solicitors and others allowed a liberal commission.

European.—A liberal allowance is made

to professional and other persons bringing business to the office.

IMPERIAL.—A commission is allowed to solicitors, agents, and brokers, procuring life assurances.

MEDICO-CLERICAL.—Attornies, brokers, and agents, bringing business to this office, will receive a liberal commission.

LAW LIFE ASSOCIATION.—In the circulars forwarded to solicitors, on the formation of this institution, one of the inducements was a *liberal commission.*

PELICAN.—21st July, 1824, sittings after term, at Westminster, Maynard *versus* Rhode and others, directors of the Pelican Assurance Company.

Mr. Crouch, who had been a clerk to the Pelican for twelve years, examined.

"They gave to annuity agents and others, who brought assurances to their office, five per cent. on the first and every subsequent payment."

If to this list were added the names of those offices which *privately* follow the same practice, it would be greatly increased; indeed, the exceptions are very few. The consequences of such a system are to corrupt and debase those through whom it is carried on, and frequently to increase a distress which would have been mitigated by a more honourable system. The following is one out of a thousand similar instances.

A clergyman, in order to provide at his death for a numerous family, succeeded, by great economy, in saving from his income sufficient to assure his life for 2000*l.*; being unacquainted with business, he unfortunately trusted the choice of the office at which he assured to the attorney whom he had been in the habit of employing. The attorney effected the policy at one of those offices which make no return of any part of the profits, and which, notwithstanding, charge the same prices as the Equitable. During about twenty years he received a commission* of five per cent.

* I do not recollect the precise age in this case, but it may be worth inquiring the profit derived by the agent from the sacrifice of his employer's interest. Supposing the clergyman's age, at the time of assuring, to have been thirty, the annual premium on his life, for an assurance of 2000*l.*, would be, at the Equitable, as well as at the other office, 53*l.* 8*s.* 4*d.*, out of which the agent received annually five per cent., or 2*l.* 13*s.* 5*d.*; so that his whole

from the office, which was paid out of the annual sum, with difficulty spared from the scanty income of his employer: and on the death of the clergyman his seven surviving orphans received from the office the original sum assured, 2000*l*., instead of about 3200*l*., which they might have received from the Equitable, had not the bribe, held out by the other office, been too great for the integrity of their father's solicitor. In contemplating with scorn the mercenary agent who betrayed, for so trifling a sum, the confidence reposed in him by his client, whose distressed family were thus deprived of 1200*l*., ought not some portion of our indignation to be reserved for those who tempted him to this breach of trust? What would be the sentiments and conduct of the directors of such a company, if, on some other occasion, they were to detect the same attorney offering, to one of their own agents, ten per cent., to induce him to accept for the office a bad life? Yet this would be one of the natural results of that line of con-

profit amounted to little more than 50*l*., whilst the loss to his employer's family was 1200*l*.

duct, into which they had themselves first introduced him; and whatever difference the law might find between the two cases, the moral turpitude is not very different: the company offer to every agent in the country a temptation to commit a breach of trust; their disciple and humble imitator limits his temptation to an individual.

The only circumstances urged in extenuation of this practice (for it is looked upon with regret by many of those who think themselves compelled to follow it) are, that all the offices do the same thing, and consequently, if any one were to refuse, that office would lie under a disadvantage in getting business. It has also been contended that, by giving a commission, the person receiving it is *ipso facto* constituted the agent of the giver, and that there is no impropriety in paying your own agent any sum agreed upon. With respect to the first of these arguments, it is not correct to say that all offices adopt the same system; three can certainly be named, the Amicable, the Equitable, and the Economic, which do not;* and it has not been stated that either of those offices complain of a deficiency of business. Besides, the same principle would require all offices to allow an equal commission; (in which case there could be no necessity for any;) and, on referring to the extracts made in pages 134 and 135, it seems evidently to be the intention of some of the offices to raise a belief that they allow a much larger commission than others. With regard to the other argument, (if it deserve the name of one,) it is neither just nor honourable, under whatever name it may be concealed, to offer money to one who is already the

* I am happy to be able to add to this small but honourable list, the University Life Assurance Society, which, in a recent instance, preferred the risk of losing a large and valuable assurance to the disgrace of bribing an agent. If I have omitted to mention the name of any other society which is free from this reproach, I can only regret my ignorance of any other exception; and add, that the evidence which I possess of the general prevalence of this practice, induces me to believe it to be more for the interest of that office, as well as of the public, thus to call for an explicit denial; which, if properly authenticated, I should gladly introduce into a subsequent edition. It may, however, be remarked, that scarcely any thing less than a distinct denial of the practice in the printed terms of an office, can reasonably satisfy the public.

agent of another, in order to influence his judgment.

It will naturally be inquired who authorize the practice we have been reprobating, and whether the long lists of respectable names, displayed at the head of many of these institutions, are placed there only to beguile the unwary, and to lead them to suppose that the same honourable principles, which govern the directors in their private capacity, will be adhered to when they act together as a body. There are many persons thus situated, whose known integrity or high rank render it impossible for a moment to suppose, that they are aware of a practice thus carrying on in their name. Who, for instance, in looking over the prospectus of the Medical and Clerical Assurance Society, would not immediately acquit the dignified clergy, who are placed in the first page amongst the list of officers of that institution, of any knowledge of the concluding paragraph of the second? There are, perhaps, amongst the directors of the various companies, many to whom these pages may convey the first information of a practice which secretly prevails in their own offices; and which ought either to be immediately abolished, or else publicly acknowledged, and the arguments which have been brought against it refuted, or proved to be fallacious.

CHAPTER XVIII.

Miscellaneous Remarks.

In the policies granted by most of the offices to persons on their own lives, it is contracted that they shall become void if the party die by his own hands, by duelling, or by the hands of justice; the object of this provision is to prevent frauds on the office, and remove sources of dispute. It is, however, the practice, in some offices, to make allowances in cases where it is apparent that no fraud was intended, and where great hardship might otherwise be suffered: but as this generally depends on the disposition of the directors, it is scarcely subject to any general rule.*

* The Equitable pay to the representatives of a person who dies by his own hands, but not *felo de se*, if he has paid five annual premiums, a sum equal to that at which the office would have purchased his policy at the time of his death.

In those societies which are founded on the principle of mutual assurance, the possessors of policies of a certain amount, are entitled to one or more votes at the general meetings of the society; and in the case of one or two of the proprietary companies, a similar privilege is allowed. In the latter case it is of great importance, and is an improvement in their constitution which has but recently taken place.

The following are the qualifications for votes, at those offices which admit of them :—

	£.		
Equitable . .	2000	for whole term of life, after five years.	
Amicable . .	100		
London Life .	500	prior to 1817.	
	1500	after five years.	
Palladium . .	1000	after two years,	one vote.
	3000	ditto	two votes.
	5000	ditto	three votes.

Several of these societies are willing to advance money on their own policies to a certain extent, generally two-thirds of their value. This is sometimes of considerable convenience to the holders, by enabling them on any emergency to raise money, perhaps for the payment of their premiums.

Most of the societies are willing to purchase their own policies; but the prices they offer are generally regarded as very low. This probably arises in some measure from persons, who propose surrendering their policies, not making a due allowance for the risk which the society has already run, and for which it ought certainly to be paid. Thus it happens that a person who has been paying 50*l*. annually for ten years, is surprised at the small sum offered for a policy which has cost him 500*l*. He should, however, remember, that the office has run the risk of his dying during that time, which event, had it happened, would have made them losers of perhaps a 1000*l*. or 1500*l*.

A very excellent plan has been adopted by the Economic, of placing on the back of each policy the sum at which the society will purchase it, after the expiration of any number of years beyond five.

Every person who effects an insurance on the life of another, must (by 14 Geo. III. c. 48.) have an interest in the continuance of that life: and as this doctrine has been carried to its extreme limits, it becomes necessary for the public to be made acquainted with the cases which have been decided upon it, and also to be aware of those offices who are disposed to defeat a just demand, by having recourse to a *legal quibble.*

The case of Godsoll *v.* Boldero, is the most important of these. Mr. Pitt was indebted to Messrs. Godsoll, coachmakers in Long Acre, who assured his life for seven years at the Pelican office. Having paid the premiums for three years, Mr. Pitt died, which event they certified to the office, and demanded payment of the policy. Before they commenced an action against the office, Mr. Pitt's executors, having a grant from parliament, paid the debt due from him to Messrs. Godsoll. The directors of the Pelican refused to pay the amount of the policy; and on the trial it was agreed that a verdict should be entered according to the direction of the court, and a case reserved: this case was afterwards argued in the King's Bench, and the court decided that Messrs. Godsoll had not, at the time of bringing the action, a subsisting interest, and therefore could not recover; the words are, "Upon this "ground therefore that the plaintiffs had "in this case no subsisting cause of action "*in point of law*, in respect of their con- "tract, regarding it as a contract of in- "demnity."

Now, it is important to observe that the parties, at the time of making the contract, had no reference whatever to the chance of any indemnity; the office took a very high rate of premium, sufficient to cover the risk of death, and also to afford a very large profit: and this premium was calculated without taking into consideration the chance of any or all the debt in question being paid.* It was therefore rather hard in the directors, after receiving premiums for several years, to turn round, when death accidentally takes place, and say, you have entered into a contract, our part of which the courts will not assist you in compelling us to fulfil, we will therefore not pay

* This is proved from the circumstance of the office making no difference in the prices charged, (when the ages are the same,) whether a person assures his own life or that of another person.

you.* In order to enable the reader to form his own judgment, the whole of this case, as reported, is given in the Appendix. Some confusion seems to have been introduced into this case, from want of sufficiently distinguishing between an insurance on a ship and that on a life. One fact, however, should always be borne in mind. In the former case, the chance of salvage or of recapture† is always taken into account in estimating the premium, and indemnity is the object and essence of the contract. In the latter, *no such circumstance ever enters into the computation;* the premiums are always calculated from the risk, and not from the risk diminished by any circumstance which may occur after the event assured against has taken place. Indemnity then is no part of the

* One singular result of this doctrine is, that a person may make a contract, which shall become invalid at some future period, after the whole of his part is completed.

† During the late war it was not an uncommon circumstance that a ship actually taken by the enemy was insured after the fact was known. Of course a very high premium was taken, and in this case the calculations of the underwriters were formed on the chance of the vessel being recaptured.

contract, and is only a term introduced into the subject by the law.

It has been reported that one or two other offices followed the example of the Pelican, and refused the payment of policies on Mr. Pitt's life. Indifferent as bodies of men generally are to all the finer feelings which actuate individuals, it is scarcely probable that several different bodies of directors should have adopted a course so manifestly repugnant to justice. If, however, the fact be properly verified, it forms so important a consideration for those who propose assuring their lives, that it would be unpardonable (should another edition be called for) to omit mentioning the names of those offices which adopted that course.

A policy of assurance, on which many premiums have been paid, becomes a valuable property to the possessor, and is frequently disposed of by public sale; advertisements for this purpose appear daily in the newspapers. In by far the larger number of cases, those who bid for this property can have no interest in the continuance of the life on which it was granted. It is therefore of the greatest importance to them to know whether the office which granted the policy is one of those which insist on the very letter of the law, or whether it is one whose conduct is regulated by more liberal principles. An office which thus diminishes the number of competitors for the purchase of its policies, or which, more strictly speaking, destroys all competition, reduces in value the property of those who assure at it; and though it may hope to make extravagant profit by purchasing at a low rate that which its own conduct has rendered valueless to all others, yet the public will at length see through the artifice, and leave it to expire in merited neglect.

APPENDIX.

No. I.

Godsoll *and Others against* Boldero *and Others.*

This was an action of debt on a policy of insurance, made the 29th of November, 1803, under seal of the defendants, as three of the directors of the Pelican Life Assurance Company, on behalf of the company; which recited that the plaintiffs, coachmakers in Long Acre, being interested in the life of the Right Honourable William Pitt, and desirous of making an insurance thereon for seven years, had subscribed and delivered into the office of the company the usual declaration, setting forth his health and age, &c.; and having paid the premium of 15*l.* 15*s.*, as a consideration for the assurance of 500*l.* for one year, from the 28th of November, 1803: it was agreed that, in case Mr. Pitt should happen to die at any time within one year, &c. the funds of the company should be liable to pay and make good to the plaintiffs, their executors, &c., within three months after his demise should have been duly certified to the trustees, &c. the sum of 500*l.*; and further, that that policy might be continued in force from year to year, until the expiration of the term of seven years, provided the annual premium should be duly paid on or before the 28th of November in each year. The plaintiffs then averred that, at the time of making the said assurance, and from thence until the death of Mr.

Pitt, they were interested in his life to the amount of the sum insured; and that they duly paid the annual premium of 15*l.* 15*s.* before the 28th of November, 1804, and the further sum of 15*l.* 15*s.* before the 28th of November, 1805; and that, after that day, while the assurance was in force and before the exhibiting the bill of the plaintiffs, viz. on the 23d of February, 1806, Mr. Pitt died; that his demise was afterwards duly certified to the trustees, &c.; since when, more than three months have elapsed before the commencement of this suit, &c.; but that the 500*l.* had not been paid or made good to the plaintiffs. There were also counts for so much money had and received by the defendants to the plaintiff's use, and upon an account stated.

To this the defendants pleaded—1st. *Nil debent.* 2dly. That the plaintiffs, at the time of making the assurance, and from thence until the death of Mr. Pitt, were not interested in his life in manner and form as they have complained, &c. 3dly. As to the first count, that the interest of the plaintiffs in the policy, and thereby intended to be covered, was a certain debt of 500*l.* at the time of making the policy, due from Mr. Pitt to the plaintiffs, and no other; and that the said debt afterwards, and after the death of Mr. Pitt, and before the exhibiting of the plaintiffs' bill, to wit, on the 6th of March, 1806, was fully paid to the plaintiffs by the Earl of Chatham and the Lord Bishop of Lincoln, executors of the will of Mr. Pitt.

Issues were taken on the two first pleas; and as to the last, the plaintiffs, protesting that their interest in the policy thereby intended to be covered, was not the said debt mentioned in that plea to be due to them from Mr. Pitt, and no other, replied that the said debt was not afterwards, and after the death of Mr. Pitt, and before the exhibiting of their bill, fully paid to them by the Earl of Chatham and the Lord Bishop of Lincoln, executors of Mr. Pitt, in manner and form as alleged, &c.; on which also issue was joined.

The defendants paid 31*l.* into court upon the first count; and, on the trial of the cause before Lord Ellenborough, C. J. at Guildhall, it was agreed that a verdict should be entered on the several issues, according to the direction of the Court, on the following case reserved.

The policy mentioned in the declaration was duly executed, and the premiums thereon were regularly paid. Mr. Pitt, mentioned in the policy, died on the 23d of January, 1806; which event was duly certified in February, 1806, to the trustees of the Pelican Life Assurance Company. The defendants before Trinity term last, were served with process issued in this cause on the 3d of June, 1806. Mr. Pitt was indebted to the plaintiffs at the time of the execution of the policy, and from thence up to and at the time of his death above 500*l.*, and died insolvent. On the 6th of March, 1806, the executors of Mr. Pitt paid to the plaintiffs, out of the money granted by parliament for the payment of Mr. Pitt's debts, 1109*l.* 11*s.* 6*d.*, as in full for the debt due to them from Mr. Pitt.

The case was argued in the last term, by Dampier for the plaintiffs, who contended that they were entitled to recover upon this policy, notwithstanding the payment of the debt to them by Mr. Pitt's executors out of the money granted by parliament for that purpose. It is clear that a creditor has an insurable interest in the life of his debtor, and the amount of the debt is the measure of that interest: and so far the existence and legality of the debt (*Dwyer* v. *Edie*, London sittings after Hil. 1788; Park on Insur. 2d ed. 491; and 2 Marsh on Insur. 675) is necessary to the validity of the insurance in point of interest under the Stat. 14 Geo. III. c. 48; but it is not the debt *qua* debt that is insured, but the life of the debtor. It is only necessary that the interest should exist at the time of the insurance made, and continue up to the time of the death of the debtor, as it did in this case; and the sum insured having become due, and the debtor's estate insolvent, the fact of payment of the debt afterwards, by a third party, cannot be material; such payment being altogether gratuitous. The validity of the insurance depends upon its agreement with the Stat. 14 Geo. III. c. 48, which was made to prevent "insurances on lives "or other events wherein the insured shall have no "interest:" and for this purpose it enacts (§ 1.) "that no insurance shall be made by any persons, on the life of any person, &c. wherein the persons for whose use, benefit, or on whose account such policy shall be made, shall have no interest, or by way of gaming or wagering;" and it avoids every assurance made contrary to the true intent and meaning thereof.

The 2d section prohibits the making any policy on the life of any person without inserting in it the person's name interested therein; and the 3d section provides that, "in all cases where the insured hath interest in such life, &c. no greater sum shall be recovered from the insurers than the amount or value of the interest of the insured in such life," &c. Now, here it cannot be disputed but that all the requisites of the act have been complied with. The only question which can be made is upon the third section, as to the necessity of the interest continuing beyond the time of the event happening on which the insurance is stipulated to be paid, and to the commencement of the action. But the interest need only continue up to the happening of the event insured, when the cause of action arises, and that is the usual averment in actions of this sort; and the defendants, by their third plea, admit that it continued beyond that time; for they allege that the debt was paid after Mr. Pitt's death, though before the action commenced. But if it had been necessary that the interest should endure up to the time the action brought, that should have been averred; which has not been usual, and for want of which the judgments in former causes might have been arrested. The hazard was run for which the premium was received during Mr. Pitt's life; and as he died insolvent, there was then as it were a total loss: then the underwriters' liability cannot be adeemed by the voluntary payment of a third party, though through the hands of the debtor's executors. The very payment of the premium gave the plaintiffs an interest in the policy; and it could not have been in the contemplation of the legislature, when they granted the money for the payment of Mr. Pitt's debts, to adeem the risk of underwriters. In the case of insurances against fire, it never was conceived that the insurers could avail themselves, *pro tanto*, of charitable donations collected for the benefit of the sufferers. In the case of a life insurance, the premium is not calculated upon the risk of the insolvency of the person whose life is to be assured, but solely on the probability of the duration of the life. But, if the defendants' objection be well founded, every case of this sort will be resolved into an examination of the assets: of which the insurers will avail themselves, *pro tanto*, after having had the benefit of the whole premium; and this, too, at any distance of time when assets may be forthcoming after the payment of the loss. But, secondly, by the payment of the money into court, the defendants admit a continuance of the plaintiffs' interest on the policy beyond the amount of the bare debt; for it was paid in after the liquidation of the debt, and after the action commenced. And therefore the plaintiffs would be entitled to recover something. And it does not appear how the premiums received have been reduced to the amount paid into court.

Marryatt, *contra*, said that he should not now dispute the proposition, that a creditor might insure the life of his debtor since the statute; though it might have been doubted at first, whether such an interest as that in the life of another were within the contemplation of the legislature. There was an inception of the risk on the policy, and therefore the premium was properly paid; and no question can arise on the amount of it, this being an insurance on a precise sum like a valued sea policy. The only question is, whether in the event the plaintiffs have been damnified, and can call upon the assurers for any indemnification? To pursue the metaphor, the ship insured has been wrecked, but there has been a salvage which the underwriters were entitled to, and out of which the assured have been indemnified; notwithstanding which, they still claim as for a total loss, contrary to the very nature of the insurance, which is only a contract of indemnity. Admitting that the general form of the declaration in these cases may have been such as is stated, still it is competent for the underwriters to show that a salvage has been received by the assured to the whole extent of their loss; and in no case can an assured recover double satisfaction, whether from the same or any other person, as in the case of a double insurance; and therefore it is immaterial, in this case, from what hand the first satisfaction came. This principle was fully admitted in the case of *Bird* v. *Randall*,* where it was applied to a case much stronger than the present; for there, a servant having entered into articles to serve his master a certain time under a penalty, and the servant having left his service before the time by the procurement of the defendant, this court, in an action by the master to recover damages against the seducer, held that the master's having before sued the servant and recovered the penalty against him before the action brought against the seducer, (though in fact the penalty recovered was not received till after the second action commenced, but before trial,) was a bar to such further remedy; considering the amount of the penalty as ample compensation for the injury received, and that no further satisfaction could be received from any other quarter.—[Lord Ellenborough, C. J. I never could entirely comprehend the ground on which that case proceeded. It was assumed that the sum taken as the penalty from the servant, was the extreme limit of the injury sustained by the master; but there is the doubt, for the penalty might have been so limited because of the inability of the servant to undertake to pay more; and it might have been very far from an adequate compensation to the master for the injury done to him by another who seduced his servant from him. I remember, however, a similar case tried at the sittings in the court of Common Pleas, before Mr. Justice Wilson, sitting for the Chief Justice, who ruled the same point upon the dry authority of the former decision, but as it seemed to me at the time, with considerable doubt upon his mind as to the propriety of it.—Lawrence, J. I suppose the court proceeded on the

* 3 Burr. 1345, 1 Bla. 373, 387.

ground that the penalty was, by the express stipulation of the parties, made an equivalent for the loss of the service.—Lord Ellenborough. That is so as between the parties themselves; but it may admit of doubt, whether that were the fair way of considering it as against a stranger a wrong doer.]—A voluntary payment of another's debt, if accepted as such, will protect the debtor; and if so, it will equally protect an insurer under the statute. For the object of that was to prevent wager policies; but if this policy may be enforced, notwithstanding the payment of the debt, every creditor may gamble upon the life of his debtor, by way of insurance, though without any reason to doubt of his solvency; and upon his death he would be entitled to double satisfaction of his debt. If a payment out of the debtor's assets would have been a bar to this action, it cannot enter into the merits of the case to inquire by whose assistance the executors have been enabled to make the payment. The money was paid by them, and received by the plaintiffs as for the debt of Mr. Pitt. Then, 2dly, the payment of money into court on the first count only admits the contract declared on. It admits that the plaintiffs had an interest in the policy up to the death of Mr. Pitt, but not at the time of the action brought: and where a demand is illegal on the face of it, payment of the money into court does not admit it. (*Cox* v. *Parry*, 1 T. R. 464, and *Ribbans* v. *Crickett*, 1 Bos. and Pull, 264.)

[It was afterwards stated by the court, and agreed on all hands, that the payment of money into court, on the first count only, admitted the facts stated in that count.]

Dampier, in reply on the principal question, said that the facts of the case showed that this was not a wagering policy, but that the plaintiffs had an interest in it up to the extent of the sum insured; and denied that the subsequent payment of the debt, out of the grant of Parliament, was like the case of salvage on a marine policy; for that was an advantage calculated upon by the underwriters in fixing the amount of the premium, but here the solvency of the debtor formed no basis of the calculation, but only the probable duration of his life. In *Bird* v. *Randall*, (besides the doubt of the soundness of that decision,) the penalty was considered as liquidated damages to the full extent of the injury; and the judgment recovered was considered as a satisfaction in law. If in this case the plaintiffs, after recovering judgment against the underwriters, had attempted to sue Mr. Pitt's executors, the case would have been more like. This stands as the case of gratuitous payment, by third persons, of the debt of another, and not as the satisfaction of a legal demand, nor upon a stipulation to receive it as a satisfaction of the present claim. It is most like the case of a charitable donation to sufferers by fire who were partially insured.

Curia adv. vult.

Lord Ellenborough, C. J., now delivered the judgment of the court.

This was an action of debt, on a policy of insurance on the life of the late Mr. Pitt, effected by the plaintiffs, who were creditors of Mr. Pitt, for the sum of 500*l.* The defendants were directors of the Pelican Life Insurance Company, with whom that insurance was effected. [His lordship, after stating the pleadings and the case, proceeded]—This assurance, as every other to which the law gives effect, (with the exceptions only which are contained in the 2d and 3d sections of the Stat. 19 Geo. II. cap. 27,) is in its nature a contract of indemnity, as distinguished from a contract by way of gaming or wagering. The interest which the plaintiffs had in the life of Mr. Pitt was that of creditors; a description of interest which was held in several late cases to be an insurable one, and not within the prohibition of the Stat. 14 Geo. III. cap. 48, sec. 1. That interest depended on the life of Mr. Pitt, in respect of the means and of the probability of payment which the continuance of his life afforded to such creditors, and the probability of loss which resulted from his death. The event against which the indemnity was sought, by this assurance, was substantially the expected consequence of his death as affecting the interest of these individuals assured in the loss of their debt. This action is, in point of law, founded upon a supposed damnification of the plaintiffs, occasioned by his death, existing and continuing to exist at the time of the action brought; and, being so founded, it follows of course that if, before the action was brought, the damage, which was at first supposed likely to result to the creditors from the death of Mr. Pitt, were wholly obviated and prevented by the payment of his debt to them, the foundation of any action on their part, on the ground of such insurance, fails. And it is no objection to this answer that the fund out of which their debt was paid did not (as was the case in the present instance) originally belong to the executors, as a part of the assets of the deceased: for though it were derived to them *aliunde*, the debt of the testator was equally satisfied by them thereout; and the damnification of the creditors, in respect of which their action upon the insurance contract is alone maintainable, was fully obviated before their action was brought. This is agreeable to the doctrine of Lord Mansfield, in *Hamilton* v. *Mendes*. 2 Burr. 1210. The words of Lord Mansfield are, "The plaintiff's demand is for an indemnity; " his action, then, must be founded upon the nature of the " damnification, as it really is at the time the action is " brought. It is repugnant, upon a contract for indemnity, " to recover as for a total loss, when the event has decided " that the damnification in truth is an average, or, perhaps, " no loss at all." " Whatever undoes the damnification, in " the whole or in part, must operate upon the indemnity " in the same degree. It is a contradiction in terms to bring " an action for indemnity, where upon the whole event no " damage has been sustained." Upon this ground, therefore, that the plaintiffs had in this case no subsisting cause of action in point of law, in respect of their contract, regarding it as a contract of indemnity at the time of the action brought, we are of opinion that a verdict must be entered for the defendants on the first and third pleas, notwithstanding the finding in favour of the plaintiffs on the second plea.

No. II.

Table of Mortality deduced from the Experience of the Equitable Society.

Undoubtedly the best table for regulating the affairs of assurance companies, would be one formed from an enumeration of all the individuals who have been assured at all the offices: as none of the experience which has been thus acquired has been made public, we can only avail ourselves of such observations as, having been incidentally made, lead indirectly to an approximation to such a table.

In an address of Mr. Morgan to the Equitable Society, on the 24th of April, 1800, we find the following comparison between the deaths, amongst the members of that society, during thirty years, and the corresponding decrements according to the Northampton tables.

"From the age of	10 to 20	they have been as	1 to 2
do.	20 — 30	do.	1 — 2
do.	30 — 40	do.	3 — 5
do.	40 — 50	do.	3 — 5
do.	50 — 60	do.	5 — 7
do.	60 — 80	do.	4 — 5

"By this statement it appears that in every period the probabilities of life are higher in the society, or, which is the same thing, the number of deaths is less than those in the table which is made the foundation of its whole practice, and that at all ages taken together, these probabilities are in the ratio of three to two. The society, therefore, for the last thirty years, has only paid two claims, where the tables supposed that three would become due."

From this statement the Northampton tables have been corrected, so as to represent the mortality given by the experience of the Equitable Society for every ten years of human existence; and from a joint view of the tables of mortality of De Parcieux, and those formed at Carlisle, the numbers so found have been distributed over the intermediate years. In this distribution it will be found, that the numbers first deduced are slightly changed, in order to produce greater general uniformity; in all cases, however, except one, the number of deaths is slightly increased. Different computers would necessarily make some variations in the formation of such a table; if I were to recompute it, I should be inclined to make some changes towards the latter end; these I have only refrained from doing, because the production of better materials, already existing, would render the labour of comparatively small value. Mr. Gompertz has, in the Phil. Transactions for 1825, deduced a similar table from the same data; it agrees very nearly with that in the present volume; but, from the circumstance of its being deduced from an algebraical formula, it is, perhaps, a little more uniform in its decrements. It is, however, to be presumed, that the differences thus arising would lead to incomparably smaller errors than those which would result from the use of any other tables.

It is now five and twenty years since the statement referred to was first made, and in that time, additional and much more extensive information on this subject must have been collected, not only at the Equitable, but at many other offices. The value of this experience to each office can be but trifling: but if each would communicate to the public the results of its own, a mass of information would be produced which would greatly contribute to the improvement of our knowledge on this subject, and ultimately conduce to the benefit of all.

No. III.

Formulæ for the Solution of Questions.

In an appendix to Mr. Baily's treatise on annuities and assurances, the method of constructing tables, first proposed by the late Mr. Barrett, is explained, and some formulæ necessary in using them are investigated. As several of the tables at the end of this volume are computed on those principles, the following investigations are subjoined.

If a be the number of persons alive at any given age in a table of mortality; and if b, c, d, &c. be the numbers alive at 1, 2, 3, &c. years older; and z the number living at the oldest age in the tables; and if r be the amount of one pound for one year, then the values of annuities, temporary as well as deferred, may be found in the following manner:—

The value of an annuity of one pound, on any life, is equal to the sum of the present values of all the future payments, each multiplied by the chance of receiving it. The present values of one pound, payable at the end of 1, 2, 3, &c. years, supposing r to be the amount of one pound in one year, at the given rate of interest, are

$$\frac{1}{r},\ \frac{1}{r^2},\ \frac{1}{r^3},\ \ldots\ldots\ldots\ \frac{1}{r^n};$$

and the chances of a person being alive at the end of 1, 2, 3, years, &c. are

$$\frac{b}{a},\ \frac{c}{a},\ \frac{d}{a},\ \ldots\ldots\ldots\ \frac{z}{a};$$

consequently the value of an annuity on such a life is

$$= \frac{1}{a}\left\{\frac{b}{r} + \frac{c}{r^2} + \frac{d}{r^3} + \ldots\ldots\ \frac{y}{y^{n-1}} + \frac{z}{r^n}\right\}$$

n denoting the number of years from the age of the life, to the oldest life in the table.

This expression may be put into another form, better adapted for computation. It is equal to

$$\frac{1}{a\,r^n}\left\{b\,r^{n-1} + c\,r^{n-2} + d\,r^{n-3} + \ldots\ldots + y\,r + z\right\}$$

Let a be the number of persons just born, b those alive at the end of one, c those alive at the end of two years, &c; then a table must be computed, whose first column A_v is equal to $a_v\,r^{n-v}$, and whose second column B_v is equal to the sum of the last v terms of the series within the parenthesis, a_v representing the $\overline{v+1}$ the terms of the series a, b, c; d, ... z, and n the age of oldest life in the tables; hence

$$B_v = z + y\,r + \ldots\ldots + a_{v+1}\,r^{n-v-1} + a_v\,r^{n-v};$$

and $B_{v-1} = z + y\,r + \ldots\ldots + a_{v+1}\,r^{n-v-1} + a_v\,r^{n-v} + a_{v-1}\,r^{n-v+1};$

therefore $\quad B_v - B_{v-1} = a_{v-1}\,r^{n-v+1} = A_{v-1};$

or $\quad B_v - B_{v-1} = A_{v-1} \ldots\ldots\ldots (1)$

Tables IX. X. and XI. have been calculated on this principle.

The value of an annuity of one pound, on a life aged v is

$$= \frac{z + y\,r + x\,r^2 + \ldots\ldots\ a_{v+1}\,r^{n-v-1}}{a_v\,r^{n-v}} = \frac{B_{v+1}}{A_v} \ldots (2)$$

The value of an annuity on a life aged v, deferred for p years is equal to the

Value of annuity on a life aged $\overline{v+p}$ years payable at the end of p years, and multiplied by the chance of receiving that payment.

$$= \frac{B_{v+p+1}}{A_{v+p}} \times \frac{1}{r^p} \times \frac{a_{v+p}}{a_v}.$$

But $a_v = A_v\,r^{-n+v}$; hence this expression for an annuity on a life aged v, deferred for p years, becomes

$$\frac{B_{v+p+1}}{A_{v+p}} \times \frac{1}{r^p} \times \frac{A_{v+p}\,r^{-n-v-p}}{A_v\,r^{-n-v}} = \frac{B_{v+p+1}}{A_v} \ldots\ldots (3)$$

A temporary annuity

= annuity on whole life — a deferred annuity.

Hence a temporary annuity for q years on a life aged v is

$$= \frac{B_{v+1} - B_{v+q+1}}{A_v} \dots\dots\dots\dots (4)$$

These annuities are payable at the end of the year; but as it is frequently desirable, for the sake of assurances and other purposes, to know the values of the same annuities to be paid at the beginning of each year, they may be found by adding unity, or the first year's payment, to the same annuity for $p - 1$ years.

Thus the value of an annuity on a life aged v, the first payment to be made immediately is

$$= 1 + \frac{B_{v+1}}{A_v} = \frac{A_v + B_{v+1}}{A_v} = \frac{B_v}{A_v} \dots\dots (5)$$

A temporary annuity for q years, the first payment to be made immediately, is

$$= 1 + \frac{B_{v+1} - B_{v+q}}{A_v} = \frac{A_v + B_{v+1} - B_{v+q}}{A_v} = \frac{B_v - B_{v+q}}{A_v} \dots (6)$$

An annuity deferred for p years, on a life aged v, is to be paid for by q annual payments, the first to be made immediately. Let x be the value of each of the q annual payments, then

$$x \times \frac{B_v - B_{v+q}}{A_v} = \frac{B_{v+p+1}}{A_v};$$

hence $$x = \frac{B_{v+p+1}}{B_v - B_{v+q}} \dots\dots\dots\dots (7)$$

A temporary annuity for q years on a life aged v deferred for p years

= annuity on life v deferred for p years — annuity on life v deferred for $p + q$ years;

$$= \frac{B_{v+p+1}}{A_v} - \frac{B_{v+p+q+1}}{A_v} = \frac{B_{v+p+1} - B_{v+p+q+1}}{A_v} \dots\dots (8)$$

If this be paid for in s equal annual payments, the first commencing immediately; x being one of them, we have

$$x \times \frac{B_v - B_{v+s}}{A_v} = \frac{B_{v+p+1} - B_{v+p+q-1}}{A_v};$$

or

$$\frac{B_{v+p+1} - B_{v+p+q-1}}{B_v - B_{v+s}} \dots\dots\dots (9)$$

The value of an assurance of one pound on a life aged v is equal to the sum of the values of the chances of receiving it at the end of the 1st, 2d, 3d, &c. ...... years.

The present worth of one pound, to be received at the end of the first year, is $\frac{1}{r}$, and the chance of obtaining it is $\frac{a_v - a_{v+1}}{a_v}$; hence, for the 1st year, the value is $\frac{1}{r}$ $\frac{a_v - a_{v+1}}{a_v}$; for the 2d, $\frac{1}{r^2}$ $\frac{a_{v+1} - a_{v+2}}{a_v}$; for the 3d, $\frac{1}{r^3}$ $\frac{a_{v+2} - a_{v+3}}{a_v}$; ...... and the sum of these, or the value of the assurance on the whole life, is

$$\frac{(a_v - b_{s+1}) r^{n-v-1} + (a_{v+1} - a_{v+2}) r^{n-v-2} + (a_{v+1} - a_{v+3}) r^{n-v-3}}{a_v \, r_{n-v}}$$

$$= \frac{B_v - r \, B_{v+1}}{r \, A_v} \dots\dots\dots\dots\dots (10)$$

If this be paid for in q annual payments, the first to be made immediately, let x be one of them, and then

$$x \times \frac{B_v - B_{v+q}}{A_v} = \frac{B_v - r \, B_{v+1}}{A_v};$$

and $$x = \frac{1}{r} \cdot \frac{B_v - r \, B_{v+1}}{B_v - B_{v+q}} \dots\dots\dots\dots (11)$$

If $v + q$ is greater than the greatest duration of human life in the table $B_{v+q} = 0$, and the value of an assurance for the whole term of a life aged v in annual payments during its whole continuance is

$$\frac{1}{r} - \frac{B_{v+1}}{B_v} \ldots\ldots\ldots\ldots\ldots\ldots \quad (12)$$

The value of an assurance on a life aged v deferred for p years is

$$= \frac{B_{v+p} - r\,B_{v+p+1}}{r\,A_v} \ldots\ldots\ldots\ldots\ldots \quad (13)$$

If the same be paid for by q annual payments, the first commencing immediately, its value x may be found from the equation

$$x \times \frac{B_v - B_{v+q}}{A_v} = \frac{B_{v+p}\,r\,B_{v+p+1}}{r\,A_v};$$

and it is $$x = \frac{1}{r} \cdot \frac{B_{v+p} - r\,B_{v+p+1}}{B_v - B_{v+q}} \ldots\ldots \quad (14)$$

A temporary assurance for p years

= an assurance on whole life — an assurance deferred p years

$$= \frac{B_v - r\,B_{v+1}}{r\,A_v} - \frac{B_{v+p} - r\,B_{v+p+1}}{r\,A_v}$$

$$= \frac{B_v - B_{v+p} - r\,(B_{v+1} - B_{v+p+1})}{r\,A_v} \ldots\ldots\ldots \quad (15)$$

A temporary assurance for p years, paid for by q annual payments, the first immediately, is

$$\frac{B_v - B_{v+p} - r\,(B_{v+1} - B_{v+p+1})}{r\,(B_v - B_{v+q})} \ldots\ldots\ldots\ldots \quad (16)$$

And if $p = q$, it is equal to

$$\frac{1}{r} - \frac{B_{v+1} - B_{v+p+1}}{B_v - B_{v+p}} \ldots\ldots\ldots\ldots\ldots \quad (17)$$

A variety of other questions may be solved with equal facility; and the column C_n is added to some of the tables in order to afford answers to similar questions relative to increasing annuities and assurances.

No. IV.

Of the Table of Persons living beyond the Age of 100.

Table XII. is formed from a collection of one thousand seven hundred and fifty-one persons, who have reached the age of one hundred years or upwards. The greater part were selected from a work on "Human Longevity," published at Salisbury, in 1799, by James Easton: some few of the names in that volume were rejected, as occurring twice, or as being of doubtful authority, and some additions were made by myself from other sources; but they may all be considered as having died previous to the year 1800.

After the actual enumeration, it was found, as might have been expected, that the numbers opposite each age were very irregularly disposed; and in order to form them into a table adapted to any purposes of calculation, it was necessary to reduce them to some more regular progression, a circumstance which arose from the number of instances not being sufficiently large. About the ages marked by round numbers, as one hundred and ten, one hundred and twenty, and one hundred and thirty, there appeared to be more deaths than the proper allowance: but the most singular, and which deserves notice, from its not being explicable on the same principle, was the large number which occurred at the age of one hundred and two, both amongst females and males, but particularly amongst the latter. Traces of this will be found in the diminished decrement of lives at one hundred and one, and the large increase at one hundred and two, but in the original list the disproportion was much greater. In order to form the present table, one hundred and fifty was assumed as the extent of human life, although there were two or three authentic instances of persons of greater age. Commencing with this period, wherever too large a number of deaths were found in any one year, they were equalized by transferring some of them to such of the preceding years as appeared to be deficient: thus, it was imagined, the tendency to overrate the age of old people would be, in some measure, compensated. The following comparative view may be instructive:—

	Of persons who have attained	There die before	By Haller's Table.	By Easton's	By the present.
	100	110	1000	1310	1278
	110	120	60	277	330
	120	130	29	84	99
	130	140	15	26	32
	140	150	6	7	12
	150	160	1	3	
	160	170		2	
	170	above		3	
Total..	....	....	1111	1712	1751

No. V.

Table XIII. is formed from one at the end of Mr. Morgan's treatise on assurances. The number of persons assuring between given ages, is copied from that work, and the other column is formed by the successive additions of those numbers. Half the total number, or seventy-five thousand eight hundred and seventy-seven, will be found between the ages forty and fifty, and on making an interpolation, it will appear to be a little beyond the age of forty-seven,

List of Tables in the Appendix.

TABLE I.

PREMIUMS FOR ONE YEAR.

The following Offices adopt the Northampton Premiums, which are the same as the Equitable, for One and for Seven Years.

ALBION,	LAW LIFE,
ATLAS,	LONDON LIFE ASSOCIATION,
EAGLE,	PELICAN,
EXCHANGE, ROYAL,	PROVIDENT,
GLOBE,	ROCK,
IMPERIAL,	WESTMINSTER.

TABLE I.

Premiums for ONE Year.

Ages.	Alliance and Sun.	Amicable.	British Commercial.	Crown.	Economic.	Equitable.	European.	Guardian.
	£ s. d.	£ s. d.	£ s. d.	£ s d.	£ s. d.	£ s. d.	£ s. d.	£ s. d.
8 to 14		0 14 6	0 15 3			0 17 9	0 15 6	0 15 6
15	0 15 0	0 15 0	0 15 4		0 14 6	0 17 11	0 16 7	0 16 4
16	0 15 1	0 15 6	0 16 5		0 14 11	0 19 2	0 17 2	0 17 4
17	0 15 7	0 17 0	0 18 2		0 15 4	1 1 2	0 17 7	0 19 1
18	0 16 5	0 18 6	1 0 0		0 15 9	1 3 3	0 18 6	1 0 10
19	0 17 4	1 0 0	1 1 5		0 16 2	1 5 0	0 19 11	1 2 8
20	0 19 1	1 1 6	1 3 4	1 3 5	0 16 7	1 7 3	1 0 10	1 4 7
21	1 0 0	1 2 6	1 4 9	1 3 9	0 17 0	1 8 10	1 2 1	1 5 9
22	1 1 0	1 3 6	1 5 1	1 4 6	0 17 6	1 9 3	1 2 7	1 6 6
23	1 2 0	1 4 0	1 5 5	1 4 10	0 18 0	1 9 8	1 3 4	1 6 11
24	1 2 8	1 4 6	1 5 10	1 5 8	0 18 6	1 10 2	1 3 10	1 7 3
25	1 3 3	1 5 0	1 6 3	1 6 0	0 19 1	1 10 7	1 4 8	1 7 8
26	1 3 11	1 5 6	1 6 8	1 6 10	0 19 8	1 11 1	1 5 10	1 8 1
27	1 4 7	1 6 0	1 7 1	1 7 9	1 0 3	1 11 7	1 6 2	1 8 6
28	1 5 4	1 6 6	1 7 6	1 8 9	1 0 11	1 12 1	1 6 6	1 8 11
29	1 6 0	1 7 0	1 8 0	1 9 10	1 1 7	1 12 8	1 6 10	1 9 4
30	1 6 9	1 7 6	1 8 6	1 10 4	1 2 3	1 13 3	1 7 3	1 10 3
31	1 7 0	1 8 0	1 8 11	1 11 3	1 3 0	1 13 9	1 7 11	1 10 9
32	1 7 4	1 8 6	1 9 5	1 12 3	1 3 9	1 14 4	1 8 7	1 11 3
33	1 7 8	1 9 0	1 10 0	1 12 9	1 4 6	1 15 0	1 9 4	1 11 9
34	1 8 0	1 9 6	1 10 7	1 13 2	1 5 4	1 15 8	1 10 1	1 12 9
35	1 8 4	1 10 0	1 11 2	1 14 2	1 6 2	1 16 4	1 10 10	1 13 4
36	1 8 8	1 10 6	1 11 9	1 14 9	1 7 0	1 17 0	1 12 3	1 13 11
37	1 9 0	1 11 0	1 12 4	1 15 9	1 7 10	1 17 9	1 12 10	1 15 0
38	1 9 5	1 11 6	1 13 0	1 16 3	1 8 8	1 18 6	1 13 4	1 15 8
39	1 11 3	1 12 0	1 13 8	1 16 9	1 9 6	1 19 3	1 13 11	1 16 4
40	1 13 7	1 13 0	1 14 10	1 17 3	1 10 4	2 0 8	1 14 7	1 17 7
41	1 15 8	1 14 0	1 16 0	1 17 9	1 11 1	2 2 0	1 15 10	1 18 4
42	1 17 3	1 15 0	1 17 4	1 18 5	1 11 10	2 3 6	1 16 6	1 19 8
43	1 17 10	1 16 0	1 18 2	1 19 8	1 12 6	2 4 6	1 17 11	2 0 6
44	1 19 0	1 17 0	1 19 0	2 1 1	1 13 2	2 5 6	1 18 8	2 1 5
45	2 1 10	1 18 0	2 0 0	2 1 9	1 13 9	2 6 8	2 0 6	2 2 3
46	2 3 8	1 19 0	2 1 0	2 2 5	1 14 4	2 7 10	2 2 6	2 3 3
47	2 4 6	2 0 0	2 2 0	2 4 0	1 15 0	2 9 0	2 3 10	2 4 3
48	2 5 4	2 1 6	2 3 1	2 5 9	1 15 9	2 10 3	2 5 7	2 5 11
49	2 8 0	2 3 0	2 4 10	2 7 6	1 16 8	2 12 3	2 6 9	2 7 0
50	2 10 9	2 4 6	2 10 3	2 10 4	1 17 11	2 15 1	2 8 8	2 9 7
51	2 13 8	2 6 0	2 13 4	2 13 4	1 19 8	2 17 4	2 9 10	2 12 4
52	2 15 7	2 7 6	2 15 6	2 16 6	2 1 10	2 19 1	2 11 3	2 14 6
53	2 18 2	2 9 6	2 18 0	2 19 9	2 4 5	3 1 0	2 13 3	2 16 1
54	3 0 4	2 11 6	3 1 0	3 1 1	2 7 5	3 3 0	2 14 7	2 17 9
55	3 2 7	2 13 6	3 4 0	3 3 7	2 10 10	3 5 0	2 17 1	3 0 4
56	3 6 4	2 15 6	3 7 0	3 6 3	2 14 9	3 7 3	3 1 8	3 2 3
57	3 9 8	2 17 6	3 9 2	3 9 1	2 19 1	3 9 8	3 5 2	3 4 4
58	3 12 7	2 19 6	3 12 0	3 12 1	3 3 9	3 12 3	3 8 5	3 7 5
59	3 15 8	3 1 6	3 14 9	3 14 11	3 8 8	3 15 1	3 12 6	3 11 8
60	4 3 7	3 4 0	3 18 1	3 17 0	3 13 10	3 18 1	3 17 6	3 16 3
61		3 6 6				4 1 5		
62		3 9 0				4 3 11		
63		3 11 6				4 7 8		
64		3 14 6				4 10 9		
65		3 18 0				4 15 2		
66		4 2 0				5 0 1		
67		4 6 0				5 5 6		
68		4 13 6						
69		5 1 6						
70		5 10 6						

TABLE I.

Premiums for ONE Year.

Ages.	London Assurance, Birchin Lane.	Medico-Clerical.	Norwich.	Palladium.	Union.	United Empire.	University.	West of England.	Assurance at Paris.
	£ s. d.	£ s. d.	£ s. d.	£ s. d.	£ s. d.	£ s. d.	£ s. d.	£ s. d.	£ s. d.
8 to 14	0 15 6	0 17 4	0 16 0	0 15 0	0 13 6	0 15 4	0 16 11	0 16 0	0 17 10
15	0 15 9	0 17 6	0 16 2	0 15 6	0 13 8	0 16 0	0 17 1	0 16 2	0 18 10
16	0 16 10	0 18 9	0 17 3	0 16 0	0 15 0	0 17 1	0 18 3	0 17 4	0 19 7
17	0 18 7	1 0 8	0 19 0	0 17 0	0 16 10	0 18 5	1 0 2	0 19 0	1 0 7
18	1 0 5	1 2 8	1 1 0	0 19 0	0 18 0	0 19 10	1 2 2	1 1 0	1 1 7
19	1 1 10	1 4 5	1 2 6	1 1 0	0 19 1	1 1 3	1 3 9	1 2 6	1 2 7
20	1 3 10	1 6 7	1 4 6	1 3 0	1 1 0	1 3 0	1 5 11	1 4 6	1 3 7
21	1 5 2	1 8 2	1 6 0	1 5 0	1 2 1	1 4 3	1 7 5	1 6 0	1 4 5
22	1 5 7	1 8 7	1 6 6	1 7 0	1 2 11	1 5 0	1 7 10	1 6 3	1 5 2
23	1 6 0	1 9 0	1 6 10	1 8 0	1 3 1	1 5 6	1 8 3	1 6 8	1 6 0
24	1 6 6	1 9 5	1 7 3	1 9 0	1 3 5	1 6 0	1 8 8	1 7 3	1 6 10
25	1 6 9	1 9 10	1 7 8	1 10 0	1 4 1	1 6 6	1 9 1	1 7 6	1 7 7
26	1 7 2	1 10 4	1 8 0	1 10 6	1 4 7	1 7 0	1 9 7	1 8 0	1 8 5
27	1 7 7	1 10 10	1 8 6	1 11 0	1 5 0	1 7 8	1 10 1	1 8 6	1 9 0
28	1 8 0	1 11 4	1 9 0	1 12 0	1 5 4	1 8 0	1 10 6	1 8 10	1 9 7
29	1 8 8	1 11 11	1 9 8	1 12 8	1 6 0	1 8 9	1 11 1	1 9 4	1 10 5
30	1 9 1	1 12 5	1 10 2	1 13 3	1 6 5	1 9 3	1 11 8	1 10 0	1 11 0
31	1 9 6	1 12 11	1 10 8	1 13 9	1 7 1	1 9 9	1 12 1	1 10 6	1 11 7
32	1 10 0	1 13 6	1 11 3	1 14 4	1 7 6	1 10 3	1 12 8	1 11 0	1 12 2
33	1 10 8	1 14 2	1 12 0	1 15 0	1 8 0	1 10 9	1 13 3	1 11 6	1 12 10
34	1 11 4	1 14 10	1 12 8	1 15 8	1 8 5	1 11 9	1 13 11	1 12 3	1 13 5
35	1 11 9	1 15 5	1 13 4	1 16 4	1 9 1	1 12 6	1 14 7	1 12 9	1 14 2
36	1 12 5	1 16 1	1 14 0	1 17 0	1 9 5	1 13 2	1 15 2	1 13 4	1 14 9
37	1 13 0	1 17 0	1 14 9	1 17 9	1 10 0	1 14 3	1 15 11	1 14 0	1 15 5
38	1 13 3	1 18 8	1 15 6	1 18 6	1 10 6	1 14 9	1 16 7	1 14 8	1 16 2
39	1 14 4	1 19 3	1 16 3	1 19 3	1 11 0	1 15 6	1 17 4	1 15 3	1 17 0
40	1 15 8	2 0 8	1 17 2	2 0 8	1 11 10	1 16 6	1 18 8	1 16 8	1 17 9
41	1 16 9	2 2 0	1 18 6	2 2 0	1 13 1	1 17 6	1 19 11	1 17 10	1 18 9
42	1 18 1	2 3 6	1 19 10	2 3 6	1 14 1	1 18 6	2 1 4	1 19 3	1 19 9
43	1 18 11	2 4 6	2 0 10	2 4 6	1 15 1	1 19 6	2 2 4	2 0 0	2 0 9
44	1 19 10	2 5 6	2 1 6	2 5 6	1 16 1	2 0 6	2 3 3	2 1 0	2 2 0
45	2 1 0	2 6 8	2 2 4	2 6 8	1 17 1	2 1 6	2 4 4	2 2 0	2 3 2
46	2 1 9	2 7 10	2 3 4	2 7 10	1 18 1	2 2 6	2 5 6	2 3 0	2 4 9
47	2 2 11	2 9 0	2 4 6	2 9 0	1 19 0	2 3 9	2 6 7	2 4 0	2 6 2
48	2 4 0	2 10 3	2 5 8	2 10 3	2 0 6	2 5 2	2 8 0	2 5 3	2 8 0
49	2 5 9	2 12 6	2 7 6	2 12 3	2 2 1	2 6 9	2 10 2	2 7 0	2 9 9
50	2 8 2	2 15 1	2 10 0	2 15 1	2 3 7	2 8 9	2 13 2	2 9 7	2 12 0
51	2 13 8	2 18 0	2 12 10	2 17 4	2 5 1	2 11 3	2 15 8	2 11 9	2 14 2
52	2 15 4	3 0 7	2 14 8	2 19 1	2 6 7	2 13 0	2 17 8	2 13 2	2 16 7
53	2 17 2	3 2 6	2 16 6	3 1 0	2 8 7	2 14 9	2 19 10	2 15 0	2 19 2
54	2 19 1	3 4 6	2 18 6	3 3 0	2 10 6	2 16 6	3 2 1	2 16 9	3 2 2
55	3 0 11	3 6 7	3 0 6	3 5 0	2 12 6	2 18 6	3 4 5	2 18 6	3 5 4
56	3 3 0	3 8 11	3 2 6	3 7 3	2 14 6	3 0 9	3 6 11	3 0 6	3 8 9
57	3 5 5	3 11 4	3 4 6	3 9 8	2 16 6	3 3 6	3 9 8	3 2 8	3 12 7
58	3 7 9	3 14 0	3 7 0	3 12 3	3 18 7	3 6 6	3 12 3	3 5 0	3 16 9
59	3 10 4	3 16 11	3 10 0	3 15 1	3 0 5	3 10 0	3 15 1	3 7 7	4 1 2
60	3 13 2	3 19 11	3 13 0	3 18 1	3 3 1	3 13 9	3 18 1	3 10 6	4 6 0
61		4 3 5		4 1 5	3 5 6		4 1 5	3 13 5	4 13 2
62		4 6 0		4 3 11	3 7 11		4 3 11	3 15 9	4 17 0
63		4 9 10		4 7 8	3 10 4		4 7 8	3 19 0	5 3 0
64		4 13 0		4 10 9	3 13 3		4 10 9	4 1 9	5 9 10
65		4 17 6		4 15 2	3 16 0		4 15 2	4 5 9	5 17 0
66		5 3 6		5 0 1	4 1 0		5 0 1	4 10 0	6 4 10
67		5 8 1		5 5 6	4 5 1		5 5 6	4 15 0	6 13 2
68				6 0 0				5 0 3	7 2 4
69				6 15 0				5 6 6	7 12 2
70				7 12 0				5 13 6	8 3 0

TABLE II.

PREMIUMS FOR SEVEN YEARS.

The following Offices adopt the Northampton Premiums, which are the same as the Equitable for One and for Seven Years.

ALBION,	LAW LIFE,
ATLAS,	LONDON LIFE ASSOCIATION,
EAGLE,	PELICAN,
EXCHANGE, ROYAL,	PROVIDENT,
GLOBE,	ROCK,
IMPERIAL,	WESTMINSTER.

TABLE II.

Premiums for SEVEN Years.

Ages.	Alliance and Sun.	Amicable.	British Commercial.	Crown.	Economic.	Equitable.	European.	Guardian.
	£ s. d.	£ s. d.	£ s. d.		£ s. d.	£ s. d.	£ s. d.	£ s. d.
8 to 14		0 18 0	0 18 5			1 1 5	0 17 9	0 19 3
15	0 16 9	0 19 0	0 19 8		0 15 8	1 2 11	0 18 8	1 0 8
16	0 17 7	1 0 0	1 1 1		0 16 1	1 4 7	0 19 6	1 2 2
17	0 18 7	1 1 0	1 2 4		0 16 6	1 6 1	1 0 4	1 3 6
18	0 19 7	1 2 0	1 3 6		0 16 11	1 7 5	1 1 3	1 4 9
19	1 0 7	1 3 6	1 4 5		0 17 5	1 8 6	1 2 2	1 5 9
20	1 1 7	1 4 6	1 5 3	1 4 8	0 17 11	1 9 5	1 3 2	1 6 7
21	1 2 4	1 5 0	1 5 10	1 5 3	0 18 5	1 10 1	1 3 11	1 7 2
22	1 3 1	1 5 6	1 6 2	1 5 11	0 19 0	1 10 6	1 4 7	1 7 7
23	1 3 10	1 6 0	1 6 7	1 6 8	0 19 7	1 11 0	1 5 2	1 8 0
24	1 4 6	1 6 6	1 7 0	1 7 5	1 0 2	1 11 6	1 5 7	1 8 6
25	1 5 2	1 7 0	1 7 6	1 8 3	1 0 10	1 12 1	1 6 4	1 9 0
26	1 5 9	1 7 6	1 7 11	1 9 1	1 1 6	1 12 7	1 6 11	1 9 6
27	1 6 3	1 8 0	1 8 5	1 9 11	1 2 2	1 13 2	1 7 5	1 10 0
28	1 6 9	1 8 6	1 8 11	1 10 9	1 2 11	1 13 9	1 8 0	1 10 7
29	1 7 3	1 9 0	1 9 5	1 11 6	1 3 8	1 14 4	1 8 7	1 11 3
30	1 7 7	1 9 6	1 9 11	1 12 3	1 4 5	1 14 11	1 9 4	1 11 10
31	1 7 11	1 10 0	1 10 6	1 12 11	1 5 2	1 15 7	1 10 1	1 12 6
32	1 8 4	1 10 6	1 11 1	1 13 8	1 6 0	1 16 3	1 10 11	1 13 3
33	1 8 10	1 11 0	1 11 7	1 14 3	1 6 10	1 16 10	1 11 9	1 14 0
34	1 9 9	1 11 6	1 12 3	1 14 10	1 7 8	1 17 8	1 12 5	1 14 9
35	1 10 11	1 12 0	1 13 4	1 15 7	1 8 6	1 18 10	1 13 3	1 15 7
36	1 12 2	1 13 0	1 13 11	1 16 2	1 9 4	1 19 7	1 14 1	1 16 6
37	1 13 5	1 14 0	1 14 10	1 16 10	1 10 1	2 0 8	1 14 10	1 17 5
38	1 14 11	1 15 0	1 15 9	1 17 6	1 10 10	2 1 9	1 15 8	1 18 4
39	1 16 8	1 16 0	1 16 9	1 18 3	1 11 7	2 2 11	1 16 8	1 19 3
40	1 18 6	1 17 0	1 17 9	1 19 0	1 12 4	2 4 1	1 17 10	2 0 3
41	1 19 10	1 18 0	1 18 10	1 19 11	1 13 0	2 5 4	1 19 2	2 1 2
42	2 1 0	1 19 0	1 19 10	2 1 0	1 13 8	2 6 6	2 0 6	2 2 3
43	2 2 6	2 0 0	2 0 11	2 2 3	1 14 4	2 7 9	2 1 11	2 3 3
44	2 4 4	2 1 0	2 2 2	2 3 8	1 15 1	2 9 2	2 3 6	2 4 6
45	2 6 5	2 2 0	2 3 7	2 5 3	1 16 0	2 10 10	2 5 1	2 6 0
46	2 8 3	2 3 0	2 5 0	2 7 3	1 17 1	2 12 6	2 6 9	2 7 8
47	2 10 3	2 4 6	2 6 7	2 9 8	1 18 5	2 14 4	2 8 1	2 9 6
48	2 12 6	2 6 0	2 8 3	2 12 0	2 0 1	2 16 4	2 9 8	2 11 5
49	2 15 0	2 8 0	2 10 2	2 14 6	2 2 2	2 18 6	2 11 3	2 13 5
50	2 17 7	2 10 0	2 16 0	2 17 2	2 4 7	3 0 8	2 13 3	2 15 8
51	3 0 3	2 12 0	3 0 2	2 19 10	2 7 6	3 2 8	2 15 6	2 17 9
52	3 2 10	2 14 0	3 2 1	3 2 6	2 10 10	3 4 9	2 18 0	2 19 10
53	3 5 8	2 16 0	3 4 6	3 5 1	2 14 6	3 7 0	3 1 0	3 2 2
54	3 9 1	2 18 0	3 8 0	3 7 6	2 18 7	3 9 5	3 4 4	3 5 0
55	3 13 6	3 0 0	3 11 1	3 10 2	3 3 0	3 12 0	3 8 2	3 8 2
56	3 18 11	3 2 0	3 14 0	3 12 11	3 7 9	3 14 8	3 12 5	3 11 5
57	4 4 9	3 4 0	3 17 0	3 15 11	3 12 9	3 17 6	3 16 6	3 15 0
58	4 11 2	3 6 6	4 0 0	3 19 0	3 18 0	4 0 6	4 0 7	3 18 9
59	4 18 8	3 9 6	4 3 0	4 2 4	4 3 7	4 3 8	4 4 10	4 2 9
60	5 7 8	3 12 6	4 7 1	4 5 11	4 9 6	4 7 1	4 9 1	4 6 9
61		3 15 6				4 10 11		
62		3 19 0				4 15 0		
63		4 2 6				4 19 8		
64		4 7 0				5 4 10		
65		4 12 0				5 10 10		
66		4 17 6				5 17 7		
67		5 4 0				6 5 2		
68		5 13 6						
69		6 4 0						
70		6 17 6						

TABLE II.

Premiums for SEVEN Years.

Ages.	London Assurance, Birchin Lane.	Medico-Clerical.	Norwich.	Palladium.	Union.	United Empire.	University.	West of England.
8 to	£ s. d.	£ s. d.	£ s. d.	£ s. d.	£ s. d.	£ s d.	£ s. d.	£ s. d.
14	0 19 0	1 0 11	0 19 4	0 17 0	0 16 5	0 18 6	1 0 5	0 19 4
15	1 0 2	1 2 5	1 0 8	0 18 0	0 17 10	0 19 8	1 1 10	1 0 9
16	1 1 6	1 4 0	1 2 2	0 19 0	0 19 6	1 1 0	1 3 5	1 2 0
17	1 2 9	1 5 6	1 3 6	1 0 6	1 0 8	1 2 3	1 4 10	1 3 6
18	1 4 1	1 6 9	1 4 9	1 2 0	1 1 6	1 3 3	1 6 1	1 4 9
19	1 5 0	1 7 10	1 5 8	1 4 0	1 3 0	1 4 3	1 7 1	1 5 8
20	1 5 10	1 8 9	1 6 6	1 6 0	1 4 3	1 5 3	1 8 0	1 6 6
21	1 6 3	1 9 4	1 7 3	1 7 0	1 4 10	1 6 0	1 8 7	1 7 0
22	1 6 8	1 9 9	1 7 8	1 8 0	1 5 3	1 6 6	1 9 0	1 7 6
23	1 7 2	1 10 3	1 8 0	1 9 0	1 5 9	1 7 0	1 9 6	1 8 0
24	1 7 7	1 10 9	1 8 6	1 10 0	1 6 3	1 7 6	1 10 0	1 8 3
25	1 8 0	1 11 4	1 9 0	1 11 0	1 6 7	1 8 0	1 10 6	1 9 0
26	1 8 6	1 11 10	1 9 6	1 12 0	1 7 1	1 8 6	1 11 0	1 9 3
27	1 9 1	1 12 4	1 10 0	1 13 0	1 7 8	1 9 0	1 11 7	1 10 0
28	1 9 6	1 12 11	1 10 6	1 14 0	1 8 0	1 9 6	1 12 1	1 10 6
29	1 10 0	1 13 6	1 11 1	1 14 4	1 8 7	1 10 2	1 12 8	1 10 10
30	1 10 8	1 14 1	1 11 8	1 14 11	1 8 11	1 10 9	1 13 3	1 11 3
31	1 11 1	1 14 9	1 12 3	1 15 7	1 9 7	1 11 6	1 13 10	1 12 0
32	1 11 9	1 15 4	1 13 0	1 16 3	1 10 3	1 12 3	1 14 6	1 12 8
33	1 12 2	1 15 11	1 13 8	1 16 10	1 10 10	1 13 0	1 15 0	1 13 3
34	1 13 1	1 16 9	1 14 6	1 17 8	1 11 2	1 13 9	1 15 10	1 14 0
35	1 13 11	1 17 11	1 15 4	1 18 10	1 11 10	1 14 6	1 16 11	1 15 0
36	1 14 7	1 18 8	1 16 2	1 19 7	1 12 6	1 15 6	1 17 8	1 15 6
37	1 15 8	1 19 10	1 17 0	2 0 8	1 13 5	1 16 6	1 18 8	1 16 8
38	1 16 6	2 1 0	1 18 0	2 1 9	1 14 5	1 17 4	1 19 8	1 17 9
39	1 17 8	2 2 2	1 19 0	2 2 11	1 15 4	1 18 0	2 0 10	1 18 9
40	1 18 6	2 3 4	2 0 0	2 4 1	1 16 7	1 19 0	2 1 11	1 19 9
41	1 19 7	2 4 6	2 1 2	2 5 4	1 17 8	2 0 2	2 3 1	2 0 10
42	2 0 8	2 5 8	2 2 4	2 6 6	1 18 6	2 1 3	2 4 3	2 1 10
43	2 1 10	2 7 9	2 3 6	2 7 9	1 19 6	2 2 6	2 5 5	2 3 0
44	2 3 1	2 9 2	2 4 10	2 9 2	2 0 8	2 3 9	2 6 9	2 4 3
45	2 4 5	2 10 10	2 6 6	2 10 10	2 1 4	2 5 6	2 8 4	2 5 10
46	2 6 0	2 12 6	2 8 2	2 12 6	2 2 6	2 7 0	2 9 11	2 7 3
47	2 7 6	2 14 4	2 10 0	2 14 4	2 4 1	2 8 9	2 11 8	2 8 10
48	2 9 3	2 17 0	2 12 0	2 16 4	2 5 4	2 10 6	2 13 10	2 10 9
49	2 11 3	2 19 6	2 14 0	2 18 6	2 7 3	2 12 6	2 16 2	2 12 9
50	2 13 2	3 2 2	2 16 2	3 0 8	2 8 11	2 14 6	2 18 7	2 14 7
51	2 18 10	3 4 4	2 18 3	3 2 8	2 10 8	2 16 6	3 0 10	2 16 6
52	3 0 9	3 6 4	3 0 6	3 4 9	2 12 9	2 18 9	3 3 2	2 18 3
53	3 2 10	3 8 8	3 2 8	3 7 0	2 14 6	3 1 0	3 5 8	3 0 6
54	3 5 2	3 11 1	3 5 0	3 9 5	2 16 8	3 3 8	3 8 5	3 2 6
55	3 7 6	3 13 9	3 7 6	3 12 0	2 19 0	3 6 8	3 11 4	3 4 9
56	3 10 1	3 16 6	3 10 0	3 14 8	3 1 2	3 9 10	3 14 4	3 7 3
57	3 12 8	3 19 5	3 12 8	3 17 6	3 3 9	3 13 6	3 17 6	3 9 10
58	3 15 6	4 2 6	3 15 6	4 0 6	3 5 6	3 17 0	4 0 6	3 12 6
59	3 18 6	4 5 9	3 18 6	4 3 8	3 8 8	4 0 9	4 3 8	3 15 6
60	4 1 7	4 9 3	4 1 6	4 7 1	3 11 1	4 4 6	4 7 1	3 18 6
61		4 13 2		4 10 11	3 13 11		4 10 11	4 2 0
62		4 17 4		4 15 0	3 17 9		4 15 0	4 5 6
63		5 2 2		4 19 8	4 1 8		4 19 8	4 9 8
64		5 7 6		5 4 10	4 6 4		5 4 10	4 14 4
65		5 13 7		5 10 10	4 11 4		5 10 10	4 19 9
66		6 0 6		5 17 7	4 16 5		5 17 7	5 6 0
67		6 8 3		6 5 2	5 2 1		6 5 2	5 12 9
68				7 0 0				6 0 6
69				8 0 0				6 9 6
70				8 18 0				6 19 0

TABLE III.

PREMIUMS FOR WHOLE LIFE.

The following Offices use the Northampton Tables, which are the same as the Equitable for the Whole Term of Life.

ALBION,
ATLAS,
EAGLE,
EXCHANGE, ROYAL,
GLOBE,
IMPERIAL,
LAW LIFE,
LONDON LIFE ASSOCIATION, *(for Persons not Members.)*
PALLADIUM,
PELICAN,
PROVIDENT,
ROCK,
UNION,
WESTMINSTER.

Table III.

PREMIUMS FOR WHOLE LIFE.

Ages.	Alliance and Sun.	Amicable.	British Commercial.	Crown.	Economic	Equitable.	Equitable Experience, increased 30 perCent	European.	Guardian.	London Assurance Birchin Lane.
8 to	£ s. d.	£ s. d.	£ s. d.	£ s. d.	£ s. d.	£ s. d.	£ s. d.	£ s. d.	£ s. d.	£ s. d.
14		1 14 6	1 9 0	1 14 10		1 17 7	1 12 8		1 15 3	1 15 8
15	1 12 8	1 15 6	1 10 0	1 15 9	1 9 1	1 18 7	1 13 6	1 13 7	1 16 2	1 16 8
16	1 13 6	1 16 6	1 11 0	1 16 7	1 9 10	1 19 8	1 14 5	1 14 5	1 17 2	1 17 9
17	1 14 3	1 17 6	1 12 0	1 17 5	1 10 7	2 0 8	1 15 4	1 15 4	1 18 2	1 18 9
18	1 15 1	1 18 6	1 13 0	1 18 3	1 11 4	2 1 8	1 16 4	1 16 2	1 19 2	1 19 8
19	1 16 0	1 19 6	1 14 0	1 19 1	1 12 2	2 2 8	1 17 4	1 17 1	2 0 1	2 0 7
20	1 16 11	2 0 6	1 15 0	1 19 11	1 13 0	2 3 7	1 18 4	1 18 1	2 1 0	2 1 4
21	1 17 11	2 1 6	1 16 0	2 0 10	1 13 10	2 4 6	1 19 5	1 19 0	2 1 10	2 2 2
22	1 18 11	2 2 6	1 17 0	2 1 9	1 14 9	2 5 4	2 0 6	1 19 11	2 2 8	2 3 0
23	2 0 1	2 3 6	1 18 0	2 2 9	1 15 9	2 6 3	2 1 8	2 0 10	2 3 6	2 3 11
24	2 1 3	2 4 6	1 19 0	2 3 9	1 16 10	2 7 1	2 2 9	2 1 10	2 4 5	2 4 8
25	2 2 6	2 5 6	2 0 0	2 4 10	1 17 11	2 8 1	2 3 11	2 2 9	2 5 4	2 5 7
26	2 3 9	2 6 6	2 1 0	2 5 10	1 19 1	2 9 1	2 5 1	2 3 9	2 6 4	2 6 6
27	2 5 2	2 7 6	2 2 0	2 6 11	2 0 4	2 10 1	2 6 4	2 4 10	2 7 4	2 7 6
28	2 6 7	2 8 6	2 3 0	2 8 1	2 1 7	2 11 1	2 7 6	2 5 10	2 8 4	2 8 6
29	2 7 11	2 9 6	2 4 0	2 9 2	2 2 9	2 12 3	2 8 9	2 6 11	2 9 6	2 9 8
30	2 9 2	2 10 6	2 5 0	2 10 4	2 3 11	2 13 5	2 10 1	2 8 1	2 10 7	2 10 7
31	2 10 6	2 11 6	2 6 0	2 11 6	2 5 1	2 14 7	2 11 5	2 9 3	2 11 10	2 11 9
32	2 11 10	2 12 6	2 7 0	2 12 9	2 6 3	2 15 9	2 12 10	2 10 6	2 13 0	2 13 0
33	2 13 4	2 14 0	2 8 0	2 14 0	2 7 7	2 17 1	2 14 4	2 11 10	2 14 4	2 14 2
34	2 14 11	2 15 6	2 9 6	2 15 4	2 9 0	2 18 5	2 15 9	2 13 2	2 15 8	2 15 7
35	2 16 8	2 17 0	2 11 0	2 16 9	2 10 7	2 19 10	2 17 4	2 14 7	2 17 0	2 16 9
36	2 18 5	2 18 6	2 13 6	2 18 2	2 12 2	3 1 4	2 18 11	2 16 0	2 18 6	2 18 2
37	3 0 4	3 0 0	2 15 0	2 19 10	2 13 10	3 2 10	3 0 6	2 17 6	3 0 0	2 19 8
38	3 2 4	3 1 6	2 16 6	3 1 2	2 15 8	3 4 6	3 2 3	2 19 1	3 1 7	3 1 3
39	3 4 5	3 3 0	2 18 0	3 2 10	2 17 6	3 6 2	3 4 1	3 0 9	3 3 3	3 3 0
40	3 6 6	3 5 0	3 0 0	3 4 7	2 19 4	3 7 11	3 6 0	3 2 6	3 5 0	3 4 7
41	3 8 7	3 7 0	3 2 0	3 6 5	3 1 3	3 9 9	3 8 0	3 4 3	3 6 9	3 8 0
42	3 10 9	3 9 0	3 4 0	3 8 4	3 3 2	3 11 8	3 10 2	3 6 3	3 8 8	3 10 0
43	3 12 11	3 11 0	3 6 0	3 10 6	3 5 1	3 13 8	3 12 6	3 8 3	3 10 8	3 12 0
44	3 15 3	3 13 0	3 8 0	3 12 8	3 7 2	3 15 9	3 14 11	3 10 5	3 12 8	3 13 11
45	3 17 8	3 15 0	3 10 0	3 15 0	3 9 4	3 17 11	3 17 7	3 12 7	3 14 11	3 16 1
46	4 0 5	3 17 6	3 12 0	3 17 6	3 11 9	4 0 2	4 0 4	3 15 0	3 17 3	3 18 3
47	4 3 3	4 0 0	3 14 6	4 0 1	3 14 4	4 2 7	4 3 2	3 17 5	3 19 8	4 0 5
48	4 6 6	4 2 6	3 17 0	4 2 11	3 17 3	4 5 1	4 6 1	4 0 0	4 2 4	4 2 10
49	4 10 2	4 5 0	3 19 6	4 5 10	4 0 6	4 7 10	4 9 2	4 2 8	4 5 1	4 5 6
50	4 14 2	4 8 0	4 6 0	4 8 11	4 4 1	4 10 8	4 12 3	4 5 6	4 8 0	4 8 6
51	4 18 9	4 11 0	4 10 0	4 12 1	4 8 1	4 13 6	4 15 6	4 8 6	4 11 0	4 13 6
52	5 3 6	4 14 0	4 13 2	4 15 3	4 12 5	4 16 5	4 18 11	4 11 7	4 14 2	4 16 6
53	5 8 7	4 17 0	4 15 6	4 18 6	4 17 0	4 19 7	5 2 5	4 15 0	4 17 5	4 19 6
54	5 14 1	5 0 0	5 1 0	5 1 11	5 1 10	5 2 10	5 6 1	4 18 7	5 0 11	5 2 9
55	5 19 11	5 3 6	5 5 0	5 5 7	5 7 1	5 6 4	5 9 11	5 2 6	5 4 8	5 6 3
56	6 6 4	5 7 6	5 9 6	5 9 6	5 12 9	5 10 1	5 13 11	5 6 8	5 8 7	5 10 0
57	6 13 2	5 11 6	5 13 2	5 13 6	5 18 11	5 14 0	5 18 0	5 11 2	5 12 10	5 14 0
58	7 0 5	5 15 6	5 17 9	5 18 0	6 5 4	5 18 2	6 2 4	5 15 8	5 17 4	5 18 3
59	7 7 9	6 0 0	6 2 0	6 2 4	6 11 10	6 2 8	6 6 10	6 0 7	6 2 2	6 2 9
60	7 14 11	6 5 0	6 7 4	6 7 2	6 18 4	6 7 4	6 11 8	6 5 8	6 7 2	6 7 3
61		6 10 0				6 12 4	6 16 9	6 11 1		
62		6 15 6				6 17 9	7 2 2			
63		7 1 0				7 3 7	7 8 1			
64		7 7 6				7 9 10	7 14 4			
65		7 14 6				7 16 9	8 1 1			
66		8 2 0				8 4 1	8 8 4			
67		8 10 0				8 12 1	8 16 2			
68		8 19 6					9 4 9			
69		9 9 0					9 14 2			
70		9 19 6					10 4 4			

Table III.

PREMIUMS FOR WHOLE LIFE.

Ages.	London Life Association, Premiums for Members.	Medico-Clerical.	Norwich.	United Empire.	University.	West of England.	Equitable Experience 3 per Cent.	Assurance Company at Paris.	Society in Holland.	Carlisle Tables 3 per Cent.
	£ s. d.	£ s. d.	£ s. d.	£ s. d.	£ s. d.	£ s. d.	£ s. d.	£ s. d.	£ s. d.	£ s. d.
8 to 14		1 15 9	1 13 10	1 14 0	1 15 9	1 13 10	1 5 1	1 13 7	1 16 0	
15		1 16 9	1 14 9	1 14 10	1 16 8	1 14 9	1 5 9	1 14 7	1 16 0	1 6 7
16		1 17 10	1 15 9	1 15 9	1 17 9	1 15 9	1 6 6	1 15 5	1 16 0	1 7 8
17		1 18 8	1 16 9	1 16 9	1 18 8	1 16 8	1 7 2	1 16 5	1 16 0	1 7 10
18		1 19 8	1 17 8	1 17 8	1 19 7	1 17 6	1 7 11	1 17 5	1 18 0	1 8 6
19		2 0 7	1 18 6	1 18 7	2 0 7	1 18 6	1 8 9	1 18 5	2 0 0	1 9 2
20		2 1 6	1 19 6	1 19 6	2 1 5	1 19 3	1 9 6	1 19 3	2 2 0	1 9 10
21	2 4 6	2 2 5	2 0 6	2 0 5	2 2 4	2 0 0	1 10 4	2 0 2	2 4 0	1 10 7
22	2 5 6	2 3 6	2 1 3	2 1 3	2 3 1	2 0 10	1 11 2	2 1 2	2 6 0	1 11 5
23	2 6 6	2 4 6	2 2 0	2 2 1	2 4 0	2 1 3	1 12 0	2 2 2	2 8 0	1 12 3
24	2 7 0	2 5 6	2 2 9	2 3 0	2 4 9	2 2 6	1 12 11	2 3 2	2 10 0	1 13 1
25	2 8 0	2 6 6	2 3 8	2 3 11	2 5 9	2 3 3	1 13 9	2 4 2	2 12 0	1 14 1
26	2 9 0	2 7 7	2 4 8	2 4 11	2 6 8	2 4 0	1 14 8	2 5 2	2 14 0	1 15 0
27	2 10 0	2 8 7	2 5 8	2 5 11	2 7 7	2 5 0	1 15 7	2 6 5	2 16 0	1 16 0
28	2 11 0	2 9 7	2 6 8	2 7 0	2 8 7	2 6 0	1 16 7	2 7 5	2 18 0	1 17 1
29	2 12 6	2 10 9	2 7 9	2 8 1	2 9 8	2 7 0	1 17 6	2 8 7	3 0 0	1 18 1
30	2 13 6	2 11 11	2 8 10	2 9 2	2 10 9	2 8 0	1 18 6	2 9 9	3 2 0	1 19 1
31	2 14 6	2 13 3	2 10 0	2 10 4	2 11 11	2 9 0	1 19 7	2 11 0	3 4 0	2 0 0
32	2 16 0	2 14 7	2 11 1	2 11 6	2 13 0	2 10 3	2 0 8	2 12 5	3 6 0	2 1 1
33	2 17 0	2 16 0	2 12 3	2 12 9	2 14 3	2 11 6	2 1 9	2 13 10	3 8 0	2 2 2
34	2 18 6	2 17 5	2 13 6	2 14 1	2 15 6	2 12 9	2 2 11	2 15 2	3 10 0	2 3 5
35	3 0 0	2 18 11	2 14 10	2 15 6	2 16 11	2 13 10	2 4 1	2 17 2	3 12 0	2 4 8
36	3 1 6	3 0 6	2 16 2	2 16 11	2 18 4	2 15 3	2 5 3	2 18 5	3 14 0	2 6 0
37	3 3 0	3 2 1	2 17 6	2 18 4	2 19 9	2 16 8	2 6 6	3 0 0	3 16 0	2 7 5
38	3 4 6	3 3 8	2 19 0	2 19 11	3 1 4	2 18 0	2 7 10	3 1 10	3 18 0	2 8 11
39	3 6 0	3 5 4	3 0 6	3 1 6	3 2 11	2 19 6	2 9 3	3 3 7	4 0 0	2 10 5
40	3 8 0	3 7 10	3 2 0	3 3 2	3 4 7	3 1 3	2 10 9	3 5 7	4 2 0	2 12 0
41	3 10 0	3 9 9	3 3 6	3 4 10	3 6 4	3 2 10	2 12 4	3 7 7	4 4 0	2 13 7
42	3 12 0	3 11 8	3 5 2	3 6 8	3 8 1	3 4 6	2 14 0	3 10 0	4 6 0	2 15 2
43	3 14 0	3 13 8	3 7 0	3 8 8	3 10 0	3 6 4	2 15 9	3 12 2	4 8 0	2 16 9
44	3 16 0	3 15 9	3 9 0	3 10 8	3 12 0	3 8 3	2 17 8	3 14 10	4 10 0	2 18 6
45	3 18 0	3 17 11	3 11 0	3 12 10	3 14 1	3 10 3	2 19 8	3 17 5	4 12 0	3 0 4
46	4 0 0	4 0 2	3 13 8	3 15 3	3 16 2	3 12 2	3 1 9	4 0 2	4 16 0	3 2 4
47	4 2 6	4 2 7	3 16 3	3 17 9	3 18 6	3 14 6	3 3 11	4 3 2	5 0 0	3 4 6
48	4 5 0	4 5 1	3 19 6	4 0 7	4 1 4	3 16 9	3 6 3	4 6 2	5 4 0	3 6 11
49	4 8 0	4 7 10	4 2 9	4 3 6	4 4 4	3 19 3	3 8 7	4 9 7	5 8 0	3 9 6
50	4 11 0	4 10 8	4 6 0	4 6 6	4 7 6	4 1 8	3 11 0	4 13 2	5 12 0	3 12 5
51	4 14 0	4 13 11	4 9 8	4 9 9	4 10 9	4 4 3	3 13 6	4 16 10	5 16 0	3 15 8
52	4 17 0	4 17 2	4 13 3	4 13 0	4 14 1	4 6 9	3 16 1	5 0 10	6 0 0	3 19 1
53	5 0 6	5 0 7	4 17 0	4 16 5	4 17 8	4 9 9	3 18 10	5 5 0	6 6 0	4 2 10
54	5 5 0	5 4 1	5 1 0	5 0 6	5 1 4	4 12 9	4 1 7	5 9 5	6 10 0	4 6 8
55	5 9 6	5 7 8	5 5 3	5 4 6	5 5 4	4 15 9	4 4 7	5 14 2	6 16 0	4 10 11
56	5 14 0	5 12 4	5 9 6	5 8 6	5 9 7	4 19 0	4 7 7	5 19 2	7 0 0	4 15 5
57	5 19 0	5 16 3	5 13 6	5 12 6	5 14 0	5 2 6	4 10 9	6 4 7	7 8 0	5 0 4
58	6 4 0	6 0 6	5 17 6	5 17 0	5 18 2	5 6 6	4 14 1	6 10 2	7 16 0	5 5 5
59	6 9 6	6 5 1	6 2 6	6 1 9	6 2 8	5 10 6	4 17 7	6 16 2	8 4 0	5 10 8
60	6 15 0	6 9 10	6 7 3	6 7 0	6 7 4	5 14 9	5 1 3	7 2 7	8 12 0	5 15 9
61		6 16 3			6 12 4	5 19 2	5 5 2	7 9 5	9 0 0	6 0 8
62		7 1 10			6 17 9	6 4 0	5 9 5	7 16 7	9 10 0	6 5 8
63		7 7 11			7 3 7	6 9 3	5 13 11	8 4 5	10 0 0	6 11 0
64		7 14 4			7 9 10	6 15 0	5 18 9	8 12 5	10 10 0	6 17 0
65		8 1 5			7 16 9	7 1 3	6 3 11	9 1 2	11 0 0	7 3 5
66		8 10 0			8 4 1	7 7 8	6 9 6	9 10 5	11 10 0	7 10 7
67		8 19 6			8 12 1	7 14 10	6 15 6	10 0 2	12 0 0	7 18 6
68						8 2 10		10 10 7	12 10 0	8 7 3
69						8 11 2		11 1 10	13 0 0	8 17 1
70						9 0 6		11 13 7	13 10 0	9 8 0

TABLE IV.

Premiums on Assurance for whole Life by Five annual Payments.

Ages.	Economic.			Medico-Clerical.			Equitable.		
	£	s.	d.	£	s.	d.	£	s.	d.
14				8	0	10	8	9	2
15	6	7	2	8	3	8	8	12	2
16	6	9	8	8	6	6	8	15	3
17	6	12	2	8	9	7	8	18	5
18	6	14	7	8	12	4	9	1	4
19	6	17	1	8	15	0	9	4	1
20	6	19	9	8	17	5	9	6	8
21	7	2	6	9	0	8	9	9	0
22	7	5	5	9	3	4	9	11	1
23	7	8	5	9	6	0	9	13	2
24	7	11	8	9	8	0	9	15	6
25	7	15	0	9	10	0	9	17	8
26	7	18	6	9	12	6	10	0	0
27	8	2	2	9	15	6	10	2	3
28	8	5	11	9	18	6	10	4	8
29	8	9	5	10	1	7	10	7	2
30	8	12	7	10	5	0	10	9	7
31	8	15	8	10	7	9	10	12	2
32	8	18	11	10	10	6	10	14	10
33	9	2	4	10	13	3	10	17	5
34	9	6	0	10	15	11	11	0	2
35	9	9	10	10	18	8	11	2	11
36	9	13	11	11	1	7	11	5	9
37	9	18	1	11	5	6	11	8	8
38	10	2	6	11	9	6	11	11	8
39	10	7	1	11	13	6	11	14	10
40	10	11	7	11	17	6	11	18	0
41	10	15	11	12	1	3	12	1	3
42	11	0	1	12	4	6	12	4	6
43	11	4	3	12	7	9	12	7	9
44	11	8	5	12	11	0	12	11	0
45	11	12	9	12	14	5	12	14	5
46	11	17	3	12	17	11	12	17	11
47	12	1	11	13	1	6	13	1	6
48	12	7	0	13	5	3	13	5	3
49	12	12	8	13	9	3	13	9	3
50	12	19	0	13	13	8	13	13	8
51	13	5	10	13	18	2	13	17	1
52	13	12	11	14	2	8	14	0	11
53	14	0	1	14	7	8	14	4	10
54	14	7	6	14	12	8	14	8	10
55	14	15	4	14	17	8	14	13	0
56	15	3	9	15	2	6	14	17	3
57	15	12	11	15	7	7	15	1	7
58	16	2	8	15	12	2	15	6	1
59	16	12	2	15	16	10	15	10	8
60	17	0	11	16	2	4	15	15	6
61				16	8	4	16	0	2
62				16	14	4	16	5	2
63				17	0	4	16	10	4
64				17	6	9	16	15	9
65				17	12	10	17	1	7
66				18	0	6	17	7	9
67				18	9	5	17	14	2
68									
69									
70									

N.B. The Terms of the Atlas, Law Life, and University Societies, are the same as those of the Equitable.

TABLE V.

Premiums on Assurance for whole Life in One Payment.

Ages.	Equitable.	Medico-Clerical.	British Commercial.	Equitable purchase at	Equitable Experience
	£ s. d.	£ s. d.	£ s. d.	£ s. d.	£ s. d.
14	39 4 6	37 5 5	32 16 0		30 2 1
15	39 16 8	37 16 11	33 9 1	31 11 5	30 13 5
16	40 9 7	38 9 3	34 15 10	32 4 2	31 4 10
17	41 2 3	39 1 3	35 9 6	32 16 9	31 16 5
18	41 14 2	39 12 7	36 3 9	33 8 6	32 8 2
19	42 5 5	40 3 2	36 18 0	33 19 5	33 0 1
20	42 16 0	40 13 3	37 12 8	34 9 9	33 12 2
21	43 5 10	41 6 3	38 7 5	34 19 0	34 4 5
22	43 15 1	41 19 6	39 7 11	35 7 11	34 16 10
23	44 4 7	42 9 3	39 18 2	35 16 11	35 9 3
24	44 14 2	42 18 6	40 19 5	36 6 1	36 1 7
25	45 4 0	43 7 10	41 18 4	36 15 6	36 14 0
26	45 14 0	44 0 1	42 12 2	37 5 2	37 6 1
27	46 4 3	44 13 0	43 11 11	37 15 0	37 18 7
28	46 14 8	45 6 9	44 9 2	38 5 1	38 10 10
29	47 5 3	46 0 9	45 6 9	38 15 6	39 3 3
30	47 16 0	46 14 6	46 4 9	39 6 0	39 15 11
31	48 7 0	47 6 0	47 3 0	39 17 0	40 8 8
32	48 18 3	47 18 0	47 14 10	40 8 2	41 1 8
33	49 9 9	48 10 6	48 6 9	40 19 5	41 14 11
34	50 1 5	49 2 4	49 8 4	41 11 1	42 8 1
35	50 13 4	49 13 11	49 13 4	42 3 1	43 1 3
36	51 5 6	50 9 0	50 9 1	42 15 4	43 14 8
37	51 17 11	51 4 2	51 5 5	43 8 0	44 8 3
38	52 10 8	51 19 4	51 17 9	44 0 11	45 2 1
39	53 3 7	52 16 4	52 10 6	44 14 2	45 16 3
40	53 16 10	53 13 6	53 3 0	45 7 11	46 11 0
41	54 10 1	54 10 1	53 16 0	46 1 8	47 6 2
42	55 3 5	55 3 5	54 8 8	46 15 6	47 19 7
43	55 16 9	55 16 9	55 1 10	47 9 5	48 17 10
44	56 10 4	56 10 4	55 14 7	48 3 8	49 12 5
45	57 4 2	57 4 2	56 8 0	48 18 2	50 11 9
46	57 18 3	57 18 3	57 1 0	49 13 1	51 9 2
47	58 12 8	58 12 8	57 14 6	50 8 5	52 6 7
48	59 7 4	59 7 4	58 7 7	51 4 2	53 3 11
49	60 2 4	60 2 4	59 1 3	52 0 4	54 2 4
50	60 17 4	60 17 4	59 14 7	52 16 7	54 18 5
51	61 12 1	61 15 10		53 12 6	55 15 6
52	62 6 9	62 14 4		54 8 6	56 12 9
53	63 1 9	63 13 10		55 4 10	57 9 10
54	63 16 10	64 14 0		56 1 5	58 6 11
55	64 12 3	65 14 6		56 18 4	59 4 1
56	65 7 10	66 11 6		57 15 7	60 1 2
57	66 3 7	67 8 0		58 13 1	60 18 2
58	66 19 7	68 5 6		59 11 0	61 15 2
59	67 15 10	69 4 2		60 9 2	62 12 3
60	68 12 2	70 3 6		61 7 9	63 9 7
61	69 8 9	71 3 6		62 6 6	64 7 6
62	70 5 6	72 4 6		63 5 7	65 2 11
63	71 2 9	73 5 6		64 5 3	66 3 3
64	72 0 1	74 6 6		65 5 4	67 1 9
65	72 18 0	75 8 9		66 6 0	68 0 4
66	73 16 0	76 12 0		67 7 0	68 19 5
67	74 14 3	77 17 0		68 8 4	69 18 9
68				69 10 0	70 18 7
69				70 11 9	71 18 8
70				71 13 9	72 19 2

N.B. The Terms of the Atlas are the same as those of the Equitable.

TABLE VI.

Tables of the Values of Annuities.

	DE PARCIEUX'S TABLES			Equitable Experience 3 per Cent.	Carlisle Mortality 3 per Cent.
	5 per Cent.	4 per Cent.	3 per Cent.		
3	15·475	18·242	22·028		22·683
4	15·752	18·559	22·390		23·285
5	15·923	18·749	22·597		23·693
6	16·043	18·877	22·726		23·846
7	16·121	18·953	22·791		23·867
8	16·171	18·996	22·813		23·801
9	16·209	19·022	22·815		23·677
10	16·203	19·008	22·766	23·768	23·512
11	16·179	18·949	22·664	23·576	23·327
12	16·106	18·844	22·506	23·382	23·143
13	16·029	18·734	22·343	23·189	22·957
14	15·949	18·620	22·175	22·997	22·769
15	15·865	18·502	22·002	22·804	22·582
16	15·777	18·380	21·823	22·607	22·404
17	15·705	18·275	21·666	22·408	22·232
18	15·629	18·167	21·505	22·207	22·058
19	15·551	18·054	21·339	22·002	21·879
20	15·469	17·938	21·168	21·795	21·694
21	15·403	17·841	21·120	21·585	21·504
22	15·337	17·740	20·867	21·371	21·304
23	15·265	17·637	20·711	21·158	21·098
24	15·193	17·530	20·550	20·946	20·885
25	15·117	17·420	20·386	20·734	20·565
26	15·039	17·306	20·217	20·522	20·442
27	14·958	17·188	20·043	20·311	20·212
28	14·873	17·066	19·864	20·054	19·981
29	14·785	16·940	19·681	19·887	19·761
30	14·693	16·810	19·492	19·671	19·556
31	14·598	16·675	19·298	19·451	19·348
32	14·499	16·535	19·099	19·228	19·134
33	14·395	16·390	18·893	19·001	18·910
34	14·287	16;240	18·682	18·775	18·675
35	14·175	16·084	18·464	18·548	18·433
36	14·057	15·922	18·240	18·318	18·183
37	13·994	15·755	18·009	18·085	17·928
38	13·783	15·556	17·742	17·848	17·669
39	13·625	15·349	17·467	17·603	17·405
40	13·459	15·133	17·183	17·351	17·143

TABLE VI.

Tables of the Values of Annuities.

	DE PARCIEUX'S TABLES.				
	5 per Cent.	4 per Cent.	3 per Cent.	Equitable Experience 3 per Cent.	Carlisle Mortality 3 per Cent.
41	13·284	14·907	16·889	17·091	16·890
42	13·100	14·673	16·585	16·822	16·640
43	12·906	14·427	16·271	16·545	16·389
44	12·702	14·171	15·946	16·258	16·130
45	12·487	13·904	15·609	15·965	15·863
46	12·261	13·625	15·260	15·666	15·585
47	12·044	13·367	14·925	15·367	15·294
48	11·815	13·076	14·578	15·069	14·986
49	11·595	12·807	14·244	14·771	14·654
50	11·363	12·526	13·899	14·477	14·303
51	11·140	12·255	13·567	14·184	13·932
52	10·927	11·995	13·248	13·889	13·558
53	10·703	11·725	12·919	13·594	13·180
54	10·468	11·443	12·579	13·301	12·798
55	10·242	11·173	12·252	13·006	12·408
56	10·006	10·891	11·914	12·713	12·014
57	9·757	10·597	11·565	12·422	11·614
58	9·517	10·314	11·228	12·129	11·218
59	9·266	10·020	10·881	11·836	10·841
60	9·003	9·713	10·522	11·539	10·491
61	8·726	9·393	10·151	11·237	10·180
62	8·435	9·060	9·766	10·932	9·875
63	8·150	8·734	9·392	10·618	9·567
64	7·850	8·394	9·005	10·300	9·246
65	7·535	8·039	8·604	9·981	8·917
66	7·224	7·691	8·212	9·654	8·578
67	6·918	7·350	7·830	9·322	8·228
68	6·620	7·019	7·460	8·982	7·869
69	6·331	6·699	7·104	8·636	7·499
70	6·055	6·394	6·766	8·285	7·123
71	5·773	6·084	6·424	7·924	6·737
72	5·505	5·794	6·105	7·554	6·373
73	5·246	5·506	5·789	7·177	6·044
74	4·985	5·222	5·479	6·790	5·752
75	4·730	4·945	5·178	6·394	5·512
76	4·458	4·652	4·862	5·986	5·277
77	4·195	4·370	4·557	5·568	5·059
78	3·948	4·105	4·273	5·147	4·838
79	3·694	3·834	3·984	4·727	4·592
80	3·471	3·596	3·730	4·314	4·365

TABLE VII.

Profit per Cent. added to the true Value of the Risks by various Offices at different Ages of Life.

INTEREST AT 2½ PER CENT.

	Age. 20	Age. 30	Age. 40	Age. 50	Age. 60
Alliance	16·9	20·7	25·1	28·0	48·8
Amicable	28·3	23·9	22·3	19·6	20·1
British Commercial	10·8	10·4	12·9	16·9	22·3
Crown	26.4	23·5	21·5	20 9	22·1
Economic	·4·5	7·8	11·6	14·3	32·8
Equitable	38·0	31·1	27·8	23·2	22·3
European	20·6	18·0	17·6	16·2	20 7
Guardian	29·8	24·1	22·3	19·6	22·1
London Assurance	30·9	24·1	21·5	20·3	22·2
London Life Association	37·8	31·3	27·9	23·7	29 6
Medico-Clerical	31·4	27·4	27·6	23·2	24·6
Norwich Union	25·1	19·9	16·6	16·9	22·2
Sun	16·9	20·7	25·1	28·0	48·8
United Empire	25·1	20·7	24·5	17 6	22 0
University	31·1	24·6	21·5	19·1	22 3
West of England	24·3	17·8	15·2	11·0	10·2

INTEREST AT 3 PER CENT.

	Age. 20	Age. 30	Age. 40	Age. 50	Age. 60	Age. 67
Alliance	25·1	27·7	30.9	32·7	53·0	
Amicable	37·3	31·1	27·9	24·0	23·5	25·5
British Commercial	18 7	16·8	18·2	21·2	25·7	27·0
Crown	35·3	30·8	27·3	25·2	25·6	
Economic	11·9	13·9	16·9	18·5	36·6	
Equitable	47·7	38·7	33·8	27·7	25·7	27·3
European	29·1	24·8	23·1	20·5	24·1	
Guardian	38·9	31·3	27·9	24·0	25·6	
London Assurance	40·1	31·3	27·2	24·7	25·7	
London Life Association	47·5	38·9	34·1	28·2	33·3	
Medico-Clerical	40·7	34·9	33 7	27 7	28·2	
Norwich Union	33·9	26·8	22·1	21·2	25 7	
Sun	25·1	27·7	30·9	32·7	53·0	
United Empire	33·9	27·7	30·3	21·9	25·5	
University	40·4	31·8	27·3	23·2	25·7	
West of England	33·1	24·6	20·7	15·1	13·3	14·2

TABLE VII.

Profit per Cent. added to the true Value of the Risks by various Offices at different Ages of Life.

INTEREST AT 4 PER CENT.

	Age. 20	Age. 30	Age. 40	Age. 50	Age. 60
Alliance	41·5	43·2	43·3	42·0	61·2
Amicable	55·3	47·1	40·1	32·6	30·1
British Commercial	34·2	31·0	29·3	29·6	32·5
Crown	53·0	46·6	39 1	34 1	49·7
Economic	26·5	28·0	27·8	26·7	43·9
Equitable	67·1	55·6	46·3	36·7	32·5
European	46·0	40·0	34·7	28·9	30·8
Guardian	57·2	47·3	40·1	32·6	32·3
London Assurance	58·5	47·3	39·1	33·4	32·4
London Life Association	66·8	55·8	46·5	37·2	40·5
Medico-Clerical	59·1	51·2	46·1	36·7	35·1
Norwich Union	51·4	42·2	33·6	29·6	32·4
Sun	41·5	43·2	43·3	42·0	61·2
United Empire	51·4	43·2	42·6	30·4	32·2
University	58·8	47·8	39 1	31·9	32·6
West of England	50·5	39·8	32·0	23·1	19·4

INTEREST AT 5 PER CENT.

	Age. 20	Age. 30	Age. 40	Age. 50	Age. 60
Alliance	59·3	57·8	59·0	57·6	84·2
Amicable	74·8	62·1	55·4	47·3	48·6
British Commercial	51·1	44·4	43·4	43·9	51·4
Crown	72·3	61·5	54·4	48·9	51·2
Economic	42·4	38·2	41·8	39·4	64·5
Equitable	88·1	71·4	62·4	37·8	51·4
European	64·3	54·3	49·4	43·1	49·4
Guardian	77·0	62·3	55·4	47·3	51·2
London Assurance	78·4	62·3	54·4	48·1	51·3
London Life Association	87·8	71·7	62 5	52·3	60·5
Medico-Clerical	79·1	66·6	62·2	51·8	54·4
Norwich Union	70·5	56·7	48·2	44·0	51·3
Sun	59·3	57·8	59·0	57·0	84·2
United Empire	70·5	57·7	58·2	44·8	51·0
University	78·8	62·9	54·4	46·5	51·4
West of England	69·4	54·1	46·4	36·7	36·4

TABLE VIII.

Table of Mortality, deduced from the Experience of the Equitable Society.

Age.	Numbers.	Difference.	Age.	Numbers.	Difference.	Age.	Numbers.	Difference.
10	6460		40	5117	62	70	2487	109
11	6435	25	41	5055	62	71	2378	109
12	6409	26	42	4993	62	72	2269	109
13	6381	28	43	4931	62	73	2159	110
14	6351	30	44	4869	62	74	2049	110
15	6320	31	45	4806	63	75	1938	111
16	6288	32	46	4742	64	76	1827	111
17	6255	33	47	4675	67	77	1715	112
18	6221	34	48	4605	70	78	1600	115
19	6186	35	49	4532	73	79	1481	119
20	6150	36	50	4455	77	80	1357	124
21	6113	37	51	4375	80	81	1219	138
22	6075	38	52	4293	82	82	1069	150
23	6035	40	53	4208	85	83	923	146
24	5993	42	54	4120	88	84	783	140
25	5949	44	55	4030	90	85	651	132
26	5903	46	56	3937	93	86	527	124
27	5855	48	57	3841	96	87	413	114
28	5805	50	58	3743	98	88	315	98
29	5754	51	59	3643	100	89	235	80
30	5702	52	60	3542	101	90	170	65
31	5649	53	61	3440	102	91	120	50
32	5595	54	62	3337	103	92	84	36
33	5540	55	63	3234	103	93	56	28
34	5483	57	64	3130	104	94	35	21
35	5424	59	65	3024	106	95	20	15
36	5364	60	66	2918	106	96	10	10
37	5303	61	67	2811	107	97	4	6
38	5241	62	68	2704	107	98	1	3
39	5179	62	69	2596	108	99	0	1

TABLE IX.

EQUITABLE EXPERIENCE $2\frac{1}{2}$ PER CENT.

TABLE IX.

Equitable Experience $2\frac{1}{2}$ per Cent.

	A_n	B_n		$\log A_n$	$\log B_n$
98	1·0000	1·0000	98	·0000000	·0000000
97	4·1000	5·1000	97	·6127839	·7075702
96	10·5063	15·6063	96	1·0214477	1·1932999
95	21·5378	37·1441	95	1·3332016	1·5698899
94	38·6335	75·7776	94	1·5869635	1·8795408
93	63·3589	139·1365	93	1·8018073	2·1434412
92	97·4143	236·5508	92	1·9886225	2·3739245
91	142·642	379·192	91	2·1542483	2·5788592
90	207·128	586·320	90	2·3162398	2·7681347
89	293·483	879·803	89	2·4675827	2·9443855
88	403·227	1283·030	88	2·6055493	3·1082368
87	541·892	1824·922	87	2·7339126	3·2612443
86	708·756	2533·678	86	2·8504970	3·4037515
85	897·410	3431·088	85	2·9529913	3·5354319
84	1106·36	4537·44	84	3·0438959	3·6568109
83	1336·78	5874·22	83	3·1260597	3·7689502
82	1586·94	7461·16	82	3·2005595	3·8728064
81	1854·85	9316·01	81	3·2683094	3·9692300
80	2116·46	11432·47	80	3·3256094	4·0581402
79	2367·60	13800·07	79	3·3743085	4·1398813
78	2621·79	16421·86	78	3·4185973	4·2154223
77	2880·48	19302·34	77	3·4594653	4·2856100
76	3145·31	22447·65	76	3·4976635	4·3511709
75	3419·82	25867·47	75	3·5340027	4·4127540
74	3706·08	29573·55	74	3·5689148	4·4709035
73	4002·66	33576·21	73	3·6023492	4·5260317
72	4311·76	37887·97	72	3·6346550	4·5785014
71	4631·87	42519·84	71	3·6657563	4·6285916
70	4965·28	47485·12	70	3·6959440	4·6765575
69	5312·47	52797·59	69	3·7252968	4·7226140
68	5671·82	58469·41	68	3·7537227	4·7669288
67	6043·67	64513·08	67	3·7813006	4·8096477
66	6430·56	70943·64	66	3·8082490	4·8509134
65	6830·77	77774·41	65	3·8344694	4·8908367
64	7246·96	85021·37	64	3·8601557	4·9295282
63	7674·95	92696·32	63	3·8850753	4·9670625
62	8117·37	100813·69	62	3·9094154	5·0035192
61	8577.12	109390·81	61	3·9333414	5·0389808
60	9052·23	118443·04	60	3·9567555	5·0735094
59	9543·11	127986·15	59	3·9796900	5·1071627
58	10050·2	138036·3	58	4·0021744	5·1399935
57	10571·2	148607·5	57	4·0241228	5·1720407
56	11106·3	159713·8	56	4·0455677	5·2033425
55	11652·8	171366·6	55	4·0664312	5·2339262

TABLE IX.

Equitable Experience 2½ per Cent.

	A_n	B_n		$\log A_n$	$\log B_n$
54	12210·9	183577·5	54	4·0867473	5·2638194
53	12783·5	196361·0	53	4·1066496	5·2930552
52	13367·8	209728·8	52	4·1260587	5·3216581
51	13963·7	223692·5	51	4·1449998	5·3496515
50	14574·5	238267·0	50	4·1635932	5.3770638
49	15197·0	253464·0	49	4·1817593	5·4039163
48	15827·9	269291·9	48	4·1994229	5·4302233
47	16470·2	285762·1	47	4·2166987	5·4560046
46	17123·9	302886·0	46	4·2336025	5·4812792
45	17788·7	320674·7	45	4·2501487	5·5060647
44	18472·6	339147·3	44	4·2665285	5·5303884
43	19175·5	358322·8	43	4·2827476	5·5542744
42	19902·0	378224·8	42	4·2988981	5·5777500
41	20652·9	398877·7	41	4·3149815	5·6008398
40	21428·9	420306·6	40	4·3309996	5·6235662
39	22230·7	442537·3	39	4·3469540	5·6459499
38	23059·3	465596·6	38	4·3628461	5·6680098
37	23915·4	489512·0	37	4·3786774	5·6897634
36	24795·2	514307·2	36	4·3943685	5·7112227
35	25699·4	540006·6	35	4·4099232	5·7323992
34	26628·4	566635·0	34	4·4253456	5·7533035
33	27577·9	594212·9	33	4·4405611	5·7739422
32	28547·9	622760·8	32	4·4555752	5·7943213
31	29544·0	652304·8	31	4·4704706	5·8144506
30	30566·8	682871·6	30	4·4852500	5·8343390
29	31616·7	714488·3	29	4·4999166	5·8539952
28	32694·4	747182·7	28	4·5144728	5·8734268
27	33800·4	780983·1	27	4·5289213	5·8926417
26	34929·4	815912·5	26	4·5431911	5·9116437
25	36081·6	851994·1	25	4·5572862	5·9304367
24	37257·2	889251·3	24	4·5712103	5·9490245
23	38456·3	927707·6	23	4·5849672	5·9674111
22	39678·9	967386·5	22	4·5985601	5·9856000
21	40925·3	1008311·8	21	4·6119920	6·0035945
20	42202·3	1050514·1	20	4·6253366	6·0214020
19	43510·6	1094024·7	19	4·6385953	6·0390269
18	44850·7	1138875·4	18	4·6517694	6·0564764
17	46223·2	1185098·6	17	4·6648604	6·0737544
16	47628·8	1232727·4	16	4·6778695	6·0908670
15	49067·9	1281795·3	15	4·6907979	6·1078185
14	50541·4	1332336·7	14	4·7036468	6·1246138
13	52049·6	1384386·3	13	4·7164173	6·1412572
12	53584·9	1437971·2	12	4·7290427	6·1577501
11	55147·4	1493118·6	11	4·7415249	6·1740941
10	56745·7	1549864·3	10	4·7539327	6·1902937

TABLE X.

Equitable Experience 3 per Cent.

	A_n	B_n	C_n		$\log A_n$	$\log B_n$	$\log C_n$
98	1·000	1·000	1·000	98	·0000000	·0000000	·0000000
97	4·120	5·120	6·120	97	·6148972	·7092700	·7867514
96	10·609	15·729	21·849	96	1·0256744	1·1967011	1·3394316
95	21·854	37·583	59·432	95	1·3395417	1·5749914	1·7740203
94	39·392	76·975	136·407	94	1·5954169	1·8863497	2·1348368
93	64·919	141·894	278·301	93	1·8123741	2·1519641	2·4445148
92	100·300	242·194	520·495	92	2·0013026	2·3841634	2·7164166
91	147·585	389·779	910·274	91	2·1690418	2·5908185	2·9591721
90	215·351	605·130	1515·404	90	2·3331467	2·7818487	3·1805285
89	306·622	911·752	2427·156	89	2·4866029	2·9598768	3·3850978
88	423·334	1335·086	3762·242	88	2·6266828	3·1255094	3·5754467
87	571·689	1906·775	5669·017	87	2·7571596	3·2802995	3·7535078
86	751·376	2658·151	832·7168	86	2·8758573	3·4245795	3·9204973
85	956·015	3614·166	11941·334	85	2·9804649	3·5580080	4·0770528
84	1184·36	4798·52	16739·85	84	3·0734829	3·6811073	4·2237516
83	1438·00	6236·52	22976·37	83	3·1577601	3·7949423	4·3612814
82	1715·43	7951·95	30928·32	82	3·2343733	3·9004737	4·4903563
81	2014·82	9966·77	40895·09	81	3·3042365	3·9985545	4·6116712
80	2310·20	12276·97	53172·06	80	3·3636498	4·0890914	4·7256835
79	2596·94	14873·91	68045·97	79	3·4144624	4·1724251	4·8328025
78	2889·78	17763·69	85809·66	78	3·4608645	4·2495331	4·9335361
77	3190·40	20954·09	106763·75	77	3·5038458	4·3212690	5·0284238
76	3500·72	24454·81	131218·56	76	3·5441574	4·3883641	5·1179952
75	3824·81	28279·62	159498·18	75	3·5826100	4·4514732	5·2027556
74	4165·19	32444·81	191942·99	74	3·6196354	4·5111451	5·2831720
73	4520·47	36965·28	228908·27	73	3·6551832	4·5677940	5·3596614
72	4893·30	41858·58	270766·85	72	3·6896023	4·6217847	5·4483457
71	5282·23	47140·81	317907·66	71	3·7228170	4·6733970	5·5023009
70	5690·08	52830·89	370738·55	70	3·7551181	4·7228879	5·5690677
69	6117·64	58948·53	429687·08	69	37·865842	4·7704728	5·6331522
68	6563·32	65511·85	495198·93	68	3·8171234	4·8163196	5·6947797
67	7027·73	72539·58	567738·51	67	3·8468148	4·8605746	5·7541483
66	7514·09	80053·67	647792·18	66	3·8758765	4·9033808	5·8114357
65	8020·66	88074·33	735866·51	65	3·9042102	4·9448492	5·8667990
64	8550·86	96625·19	832491·70	64	3·9320099	4·9850904	5·9203799
63	9100·03	105725·22	938216·92	63	3·9590429	5·0241779	5·9723033
62	9671·55	115396·77	1053613·69	62	3·9854963	5·0621933	6·0226813
61	10269·2	125665·9	1179279·5	61	4·0115357	5·0992174	6·0716168
60	10890·9	136556·8	1315836·3	60	4·0370631	5·1353132	6·1192019
59	11537·5	148094·3	1463930·6	59	4·0621110	5·1705375	6·1655203
58	12209·8	160304·1	1624234·7	58	4·0867088	5·2049444	6·2106486
57	12905·4	173209·5	1797444·2	57	4·1107705	5·2385719	6·2546554
56	13624·8	186834·3	1984278·5	56	4·1343288	5·2714559	6·2976025
55	14365·0	201199·3	2185477·8	55	4·1573057	5·3036258	6·3395462
54	15126·4	216325·7	2401803·5	54	4·1797351	5·3351082	6·3805373

TABLE X.

Equitable Experience 3 per Cent.

	A_n	B_n	C_n		log A_n	log B_n	log C_n
53	15912·9	232238·6	2634042·1	53	4·2017508	5·3659345	6·4206227
52	16721·4	248960·0	2883002·1	52	4·2232732	5·3961296	6·4598449
51	17552·0	266512·0	3149514·1	51	4·2443277	5·4257167	6·4982436
50	18409·2	284921·2	3434435·3	50	4·2650345	5·4547244	6·5358553
49	19289·2	304210·4	3738645·7	49	4·2853139	5·4831735	6·5727143
48	20187·9	324398·3	4063044·0	48	4·3050908	5·5110782	6·6088515
47	21109·6	345507·9	4408551·9	47	4·3244801	5·5384580	6·6442959
46	22054·5	367562·4	4776114·3	46	4·3434972	5·5653306	6·6790747
45	23022·7	390585·1	5166699·4	45	4·3621567	5·5917156	6·7132132
44	24024·3	414609·4	5581308·8	44	4·3806499	5·6176388	6·7467360
43	25060·0	439669·4	6020978·2	43	4·3989824	5·6431259	6·7796671
42	26136·4	465805·8	6486784·0	42	4·4172462	5·6682042	6·8120295
41	27254·8	493060·6	6979844·6	41	4·4354430	5·6928998	6·8438458
40	28416·8	521477·4	7501322·0	40	4·4535744	5·7172351	6·8751378
39	29623·2	551100·6	8052422·6	39	4·4716422	5·7412304	6·9059265
38	30877·9	581978·5	8634401·1	38	4·4896477	5·7649066	6·9362323
37	32180·5	614159·0	9248560·1	37	4·5075923	5·7882808	6·9660741
36	33527·2	647686·2	9896246·3	36	4·5253967	5·8113645	6·9954705
35	34919·3	6·826055	10578851·8	35	4·5430649	5·8341695	7·0244390
34	36358·0	718963·5	11297815·3	34	4·5606006	5·8567065	7·0529946
33	37838·1	756801·6	12054616·9	33	4·5779294	5·8789817	7·0811533
32	39360·2	796161·8	12850778·7	32	4·5950569	5·9010010	7·1089290
31	40932·3	837094·1	13687872·8	31	4·6120657	5·9227743	7·1363359
30	42555·8	879649·9	14567522·7	30	4·6289585	5·9443099	7·1633856
29	44232·2	923882·1	15491404·8	29	4·6457384	5·9656165	7·1900908
28	45962·9	969845·0	16461249·8	28	4·6624079	5·9867023	7·2164626
27	47749·6	1017594·6	17478844·4	27	4·6789699	6·0075754	7·2425127
26	49585·3	1067179.9	18546024·3	26	4·6953530	6·0282379	7·2682508
25	51470·9	1118650·8	19664675·1	25	4·7115614	6·0486946	7·2936868
24	53407·1	1172057·9	20836733·0	24	4·7275989	6·0689491	7·3188295
23	55394·8	1227452·7	22064185·7	23	4·7434692	6·0890051	7·3436878
22	57434·8	1284887·5	23349073·2	22	4·7591754	6·1088656	7·3682696
21	59527·9	1344415·4	24693488·6	21	4·7747207	6·1285323	7·3925823
20	61684·9	1406100·3	26099588·9	20	4·7901786	6·1480162	7·4166336
19	63907·3	1470007·6	27569596·5	19	4·8055507	6·1673197	7·4404303
18	66196·9	1536204·5	29105801·0	18	4·8208382	6·1864492	7·4639796
17	68555·5	1604760·0	30710561·0	17	4·8360425	6·2054100	7·4872878
16	70984·7	1675744·7	32386305·7	16	4·8511649	6·2242080	7·5103613
15	73486·4	1749231·1	34135536·8	15	4·8662068	6·2428469	7·5332067
14	76062·2	1825293·3	35960830·1	14	4·8811690	6·2613328	7·5558298
13	78714·1	1904007·4	37864837·5	13	4·8960528	6·2796685	7·5782361
12	81431·3	1985438·7	39850276·2	12	4·9107916	6·2978566	7·6004313
11	84214·5	2069653·2	41919929·4	11	4·9253871	6·3158970	7·6224204
10	87077·9	2156731·1	44076660·5	10	4·9399083	6·3337958	7·6442087

TABLE XI.

Carlisle Table, 3 per Cent.

	A_n	B_n	C_n		log A_n	log B_n	log C_n
104	1·000	1·000	1·000	104	·0000000	0·0000000	·0000000
103	3·090	4·090	5·090	103	·4899585	0·6117233	·7067178
102	5·304	9·394	14·484	102	·7246444	0·9728506	1·1608885
101	7·649	17·043	31·527	101	·8836097	1·2315460	1·4986826
100	10·130	27·173	58·700	100	1·0055914	1·4341376	1·7686381
99	12·752	39·925	98·625	99	1·1055788	1·6012449	1·9939870
98	16·717	56·642	155·267	98	1·2231513	1·7531386	2·1910792
97	22·138	78·780	234·047	97	1·3451331	1·8964160	2·3693031
96	29·136	107·916	341·963	96	1·4644256	2·0330858	2·5339791
95	39·143	147·059	489·022	95	1·5926563	2·1674916	2·6893284
94	53·757	200·816	689·838	94	1·7304322	2·3027983	2·8387471
93	74·749	275·565	965·403	93	1·8736033	2·4402241	2·9847087
92	106·930	382·495	1347·898	92	2·0291080	2·5826258	3·1296573
91	154·20	536·69	1884·58	91	2·1880732	2·7297235	3·2752146
90	214·79	751·48	2636·06	90	2·3320094	2·8759174	3·4209553
89	281·99	1033·47	3669·53	89	2·4502370	3·0142987	3·5646105
88	372·29	1405·76	5075·29	88	2·5708836	3·1479113	3·7054609
87	489·24	1895·00	6970·29	87	2·6895245	3·2776092	3·8432509
86	624·79	2519·79	9490·08	86	2·7957361	3·4013644	3·9772698
85	780·31	3300·10	12790·18	85	2·8922673	3·5185271	4·1068766
84	955·43	4255·53	17045·71	84	2·9802002	3·6289537	4·2316152
83	1159·0	5414·5	22460·2	83	3·0640697	3·7335584	4·3514137
82	1389·2	6803·7	29263·9	82	3·1427569	3·8327452	4·4663322
81	1651·9	8455·6	37719·5	81	3·2179817	3·9271444	4·5765660
80	1937·3	10392·9	48112·4	80	3·2871863	4·0167378	4·6822570
79	2263·4	12656·3	60768·7	79	3·3547563	4·1023067	4·7836799
78	2615·9	15272·2	76040·9	78	3·4176286	4·1839015	4·8810473
77	3018·7	18290·9	94331·8	77	3·4798246	4·2622349	4·9746581
76	3466·2	21757·1	112622·7	76	3·5398549	4·3376010	5·0516260
75	3947·3	25704·4	134379·8	75	3·5962943	4·4100075	5·1283341
74	4468·6	30173·0	160084·2	74	3·6501705	4·4796185	5·2043485
73	4992·7	3516·57	190257·2	73	3·6983321	4·5461193	5·2793412
72	5518·4	40684·1	225422·9	72	3·7418134	4·6094247	5·3529980
71	6039·4	46723·5	266107·0	71	3·7809914	4·6695354	5·4250563
70	6559·3	53282·8	312830·5	70	3·8168578	4·7265871	5·4953091
69	7105·0	60387·8	366113·3	69	3·8515643	4·7809492	5·5636156
68	7674·7	68062·5	426501·1	68	3·8850581	4·8329079	5·6299201
67	8272·1	76334·6	494563·6	67	3·9176138	4·8827214	5·6942221
66	8898·4	85233·0	570898·2	66	3·9493130	4·9306078	5·7565588
65	9558·1	94791·1	656131·2	65	3·9803710	4·9767676	5·8169907
64	10253·	105044·	750922·3	64	4·0108334	5·0213713	5·8755951
63	10980·	116024·	855966·	63	4·0406082	5·0645477	5·9324566
62	11749·	127773·	971990·	62	4·0700032	5·1064391	5·9876618
61	12551·	140324·	1099763·	61	4·0986667	5·1471321	6·0412995
60	13375·	153699·	1240087·	60	4·1262971	5·1866709	6·0934522
59	14177·	167876·	1393786·	59	4·1515905	5·2249887	6·1441962
58	14965·	182841·	1561662·	58	4·1750697	5·2620736	6·1935871
57	15743·	198584·	1744503·	57	4·1970786	5·2979443	6·2416718
56	16529·	215113·	1943087·	56	4·2182468	5·3326667	6·2884922
55	17336·	232449·	2158200·	55	4·2389384	5·3663277	6·3340917
54	18162·	250611·	2390649·	54	4·2591761	5·3990001	6·3785158
53	19014·	269625·	2641260·	53	4·2790837	5·4307602	6·4218111
52	19887·	289512·	2910885·	52	4·2985734	5·4616666	6·4640252

TABLE XI.

Carlisle Table, 3 per Cent.

	A_n	B_n	C_n		log A_n	log B_n	log C_n
51	20781·	310293·	3200397·	51	4·3176624	5·4917720	6·5052039
50	21695·	331988·	3510690·	50	4·3363666	5·5211224	6·5453925
49	22656·	354644·	3842678·	49	4·3551875	5·5497926	6·5846341
48	23666·	378310·	4197322·	48	4·3741191	5·5778478	6·6229723
47	24737·	403047·	4551966·	47	4·3933452	5·6053557	6·6581990
46	25862·	428909·	4930276·	46	4·4126652	5·6323651	6·6928712
45	27038·	455947·	5333323·	45	4·4319819	5·6589144	6·7269978
44	28268·	484215·	5762232·	44	4·4512937	5·6850383	6·7605908
43	29547·	513762·	6218179·	43	4·4705105	5·7107620	6·7936633
42	30877·	544639·	6702394·	42	4·4896348	5·7361087	6·8262301
41	32248·	576887·	7216156·	41	4·5084962	5·7610908	6·8583059
40	33652·	610539·	7760795·	40	4·5270184	5·7857134	6·8899062
39	35079·	645618·	8337682·	39	4·5450446	5·8099756	6·9210454
38	36539·	682157·	8948221·	38	4·5627587	5·8338844	6·9517368
37	38048·	720205·	9593839·	37	4·5803361	5·8574561	6·9819925
36	39608·	759813·	10275996·	36	4·5977804	5·8807067	7·0118242
35	41219·	801032·	10996201·	35	4·6150953	5·9036499	7·0412427
34	42891·	843923·	11756014·	34	4·6323645	5·9263028	7·0702600
33	44626·	888549·	12557046·	33	4·6495891	5·9486814	7·0988873
32	46435·	934984·	13400969·	32	4·6668482	5·9708041	7·1271361
31	48322·	983306·	14289518·	31	4·6841406	5·9926886	7·1550173
30	50279·	1033585·	15224502·	30	4·7013877	6·0143472	7·1825431
29	52302·	1085887·	16207808·	29	4·7185143	6·0357845	7·2097242
28	54343·	1140230·	17241393·	28	4·7351459	6·0569922	7·2365724
27	56412·	1196642·	18327280·	27	4·7513698	6·0779644	7·2630980
26	58535·	1255177·	19467510·	26	4·7674188	6·0987047	7·2893104
25	60736·	1315913·	20664152·	25	4·7834443	6·1192273	7·3152176
24	63005·	1378918·	21919329·	24	4·7993731	6·1395385	7·3408270
23	65355·	1444273·	23235242·	23	4·8152800	6·1596491	7·3661472
22	67790·	1512063·	24614160·	22	4·8311654	6·1795697	7·3911851
21	70312·	1582375·	26058433·	21	4·8470297	6·1993095	7·4159483
20	72936·	1655311·	27570496·	20	4·8629442	6·2188796	7·4404445
19	75655·	1730966·	29152871·	19	4·8788371	6·2382884	7·4646815
18	78471·	1809437·	30735246·	18	4·8947086	6·2575435	7·4876366
17	81388·	1890825·	32390557·	17	4·9105591	6·2766514	7·5104183
16	84395·	1975220·	34121523·	16	4·9263195	6·2956155	7·5330285
15	87469·	2062689·	35930960·	15	4·9418535	6·3144338	7·5554688
14	90593·	2153282·	37821785·	14	4·9570968	6·3331010	7·5777420
13	93797·	2247079·	39797005·	13	4·9721905	6·3516185	7·5998503
12	97097·	2344176·	41859694·	12	4·9872047	6·3699902	7·6217959
11	100494·	2444670·	44012976·	11	5·0021404	6·3882203	7·6435807
10	103976·	2548646·	46260055·	10	5·0169316	6·4063095	7·6652061
9	107642·	2656288·	48604231·	9	5·0319817	6·4242751	7·6866741
8	111605·	2767893·	51048901·	8	5·0476856	6·4421494	7·7079864
7	115974·	2883867·	53597547·	7	5·0643597	6·4599752	7·7291449
6	120938·	3004805·	56253835·	6	5·0825643	6·4778163	7·7501521
5	126824·	3131629·	59021728·	5	5·1032025	6·4957703	7·7710120
4	134492·	3266121·	61905595·	4	5·1286964	6·5140323	7·7917298
3	143990·	3410111·	64910400·	3	5·1583330	6·5327685	7·8123143
2	158606·	3568717·	68042029·	2	5·2003207	6·5525121	7·8327772
1	177687·	3746404·	71308150·	1	5·2496559	6·5736146	7·8531392
0	216307·	3962711·	74718261·	0	5·3350714	6·5979924	7·8734268

TABLE XII.

Table of 1751 *Persons reaching the Age of* 100 *and upwards.*

Ages.	Die in the next Year.	Number alive.
100	164	1751
101	145	1587
102	162	1442
103	154	1280
104	150	1126
105	140	976
106	120	836
107	94	716
108	80	622
109	69	542
110	57	473
111	48	416
112	40	368
113	34	328
114	31	294
115	29	263
116	25	234
117	24	209
118	22	185
119	20	163
120	17	143
121	14	126
122	13	112
123	11	99
124	9	88
125	8	79
126	8	71
127	7	63
128	6	56
129	6	50
130	5	44
131	4	39
132	4	35
133	3	31
134	3	28
135	3	25
136	3	22
137	3	19
138	2	16
139	2	14
140	2	12
141	1	10
142	1	9
143	1	8
144	1	7
145	1	6
146	1	5
147	1	4
148	1	3
149	1	2
150	1	1

TABLE XIII.

Number of Persons assuring at the Equitable Society under		Number of Persons assuring at the Equitable Society between the Ages	
20	1494	10—20	1494
30	10490	20—30	8996
40	44340	30—40	33850
50	89769	40—50	45429
60	126258	50—60	36489
70	145300	60—70	19042
Above 70	151754	70—above	6454